CABIN FEVER

dialogues with nature

ESSAYS BY

RICHARD E. CARTER

DRAWINGS BY

CAROLYN KENNEY

1995
Galde Press, Inc.
St. Paul, Minnesota 55165 U.S.A.

First Edition
First Printing, 1995

Library of Congress Cataloging-in-Publication Data

Carter, Richard E.
    Cabin fever : dialogues with nature / Richard E. Carter; drawings
by Carolyn Kenney.
        p.   cm.
    ISBN 1–880090–20–1
    1. Natural history—Wisconsin—Door County.   2. Natural
history—Illinois—Chicago Region.   3. Nature.   I. Title.
QH105.W6C37   1995
508.775'63—dc20   95–12551
                                                                CIP

Galde Press, Inc.
PO Box 65611
St. Paul, Minnesota 55165

To (and from) the Great Creator—
R.E.C. and C.K.

contents

When you come to the end of a long effort to write a book and get it out, you can't help but be aware of how many people helped along the way, and feel immense gratitude. You see the whole web of events stretching back even beyond the first conscious decision to go the whole distance.

Gathered around me at the writing desk, looking over my shoulder and offering words of encouragement, were the spirits of my writing coaches of years ago: Marcie Telander, Norb Blei, and Eloise Fink. And, during the recent years of grinding out the essays, I was fortunate enough to have trusted critics to read and comment on early drafts who made real contributions to the quality of the work. Long-time friend and naturalist Libby Hill and Professor William Howenstine in the Department of Environmental Studies at Northeastern Illinois University offered both encouragement and concrete suggestions for improvements.

Beyond the mechanics of writing and production were two people who have provided support and inspiration beyond their knowing. They are Julia Cameron, author of *The Artist's Way*, and Ramona DiDomenico, trusted friend and creator of visions.

Above all, I want to acknowledge my creative partner in this venture, Carolyn Kenney. From the very beginning, her excitement and enthusiasm for the work did so much to keep the project going. Just when the writing would bog down, it seemed another wonderful sketch would appear, saying "Yes!" to the work. Her unfailing support, focused critical comment, and belief in the book were a source of inspiration for me.

—*Richard E. Carter*

acknowledgments

The creative process can be a lonely one, facing a blank white page and seeing what you can do to improve it. It is also a mystery as much as a revelation. Many times I have thought that I don't know how the work is done; I just show up and hold the pencil. Surely college art teachers had an influence, though it has been many years since I sat in their classes—John Wilde, Danny Pierce, Laurence Rathsack.

But there was more. Illustrator/speaker Dugald Stermer advised me to go home, sharpen my pencil, and begin with something simple. The Clearing in Door County provided a place where I could come with a bound sketchbook to try something new. Interest and encouragement came from Andy Larsen, director of Riveredge Nature Center in Newberg, Wisconsin. And I, too, received creative validation from Julia Cameron and Ramona DiDomenico.

For all of this, I am truly thankful. But most of all I am grateful to my partner, Richard Carter, for both his enthusiastic support and the vision of his writings. His words resonated with the spirits of the wild creatures, places, and things that revealed their secrets to me. And his personal and written insights gave my art focus and context, as our work came together to create this book.

—*Carolyn Kenney*

acknowledgments

C. Kenney '92

introduction

*T*hese essays trace one man's experiences in seeking to heal his separation from nature. They are way points along a twenty-five year journey, snapshots of episodes that became moments of light collected into a album while illuminating a path not seen at its beginning. Though I have studied nature and the environment more formally in recent years, I make no claim to be an expert, except in my own experience. The arena of personal experience with nature is what I have addressed overall in these essays.

I believe that contemporary man suffers terribly from a loss of personal connection with nature and the earth without even being aware of his loss. Philosophers have been telling us this for ages, yet we are accelerating that separation with increasing speed in recent years. We have set ourselves *apart from* nature instead of seeing ourselves as *a part of* nature.

Unfortunately, both science and religion have contributed to this dangerous illusion, and our economic system, driven by insatiable hunger to consume, has been unencumbered by any strongly held earth ethics. In its arrogance, science has assured us that if we make a mistake, we can always fix it; if we destroy something we can make another, even better. We have become reckless, believing science can save us from any final accounting. Our traditional religions have taught us to be fruitful and multiply, to rule and subdue the earth as though we owned it. We have inherited an ethic of industry and exploitation to use the earth in any way that suits us. We have been schooled in dominion, not good stewardship. We have not been taught to love and respect that which sustains us.

While we are beginning to acquire an intellectual understanding of the consequences of environmental degradation, we still lack the underlying moral imperatives to restrain many of our abuses. As Aldo Leopold put it, "We can be ethical only in relationship to something we can see, feel, understand, love, or otherwise have faith in."

Ironically, it is the First Peoples of the world, the conquered people, the people characterized as "ignorant savages," who have some answers for us in healing our separation. Their stories, myths, and legends were a kind of poetry, as Joseph Campbell might say, attempting to explore the edge of the known and the unknown. Their legends give man a sense of his place in the world and his purpose in it.

Because native peoples accept themselves as belonging to the earth rather than the other way around, it comes naturally to them to have respect and reverence for it. While all native populations impacted the land, example after example can be found of profound understanding of how they fit into the unending web of life. This wisdom was woven into their spirituality, created an earth ethic held at the deepest level, and prevented wanton abuse. The idea of restraint toward the earth and its resources was coupled with both practicality and morality.

Currently, there is a great resurgence of interest in Native American culture, their ecological practices, and their spirituality. The special knowledge, which they and native people all over the planet possess, was acquired over centuries of living in direct contact with the earth. This knowledge and their spiritual awareness of their place in the world can help awaken us to new perspectives about our own place in the world and assist us in learning how to reconnect with nature. This is not to suggest that we play Indian, rather that we respectfully expand our culture's boundaries to embrace ancient truths, to incorporate them into our belief system.

The question for us is, can we reconnect with nature after we have been so long away, when we are barely aware of our separation? Is it possible that the great interest in Native American culture is an unconscious expression of an ancient, unmet hunger, a slow dawning awareness of the lack of lasting satisfaction from our accelerating pursuit of endless *things*? Could the passion of restoration ecology be springing from old seed banks deep within ourselves, longing for the light? And might it be that, when rescuing one of the least creatures of the earth becomes one of the most important things in our lives, we are responding to that lost part of ourselves? Are we rescuing birds, animals, rivers and landscapes, or are they rescuing us? Are they guides come to show us the way home? Are we willing to follow?

If we are ready, it may require some stretching on our part, both as individuals and as a culture. We cannot achieve re-connection through scientific study, intellectual inquiry, political action, or economic justification. All of these are important components for changing our environmental practices, but they are not enough. Even reading the powerful prose of Aldo Leopold, being moved by the dramatic photography of Ansel Adams, or captivated by wildlife art of Robert Bateman is not enough. As enriching as these activities may be, they remain abstractions for us. What is required for change at depth is the more direct, hands-on experience of nature: first contact, then re-connection at the deepest level, the heart level. Our interest could pass like a fad without lasting results.

There are two levels of learning or knowing: the intellectual level and the heart level. We are well acquainted with the former; in fact, it is considered the only valid way of knowing anything in our culture. Poorly understood and mis-defined, the heart level is usually discounted, distrusted, and considered unreliable. By heart level, I mean that sacred and profound inner depth of "knowing" where the connection with "Divine Intelligence" takes place. Down through the centuries great minds have acknowledged such a connection, yet we have been taught not to trust this center of knowingness. Only our intellects have been allowed to guide us. And look where they have taken us!

I don't ask that you change whatever it is that you may believe, or accept everything I am saying. Just reserve judgment and ask, "What if?" What if it is really true that the Universe, the earth, nature, really do try to communicate and my own rigidity or fear of ridicule has caused me to discount and bury my deeply felt encounters? Start trusting that part of you a bit and see what happens.

So, what if the earth is a living whole possessing an intelligence superior to our own, one with a spirit capable of "speaking" to us if we are open to it? Like many native peoples, can we begin to form a relationship with nature that gives us a confidence of belonging, of having a place in a system of continual renewal?

The essays and drawings that follow reflect this perspective. They are personal encounters with nature and environmental issues. Some are set in Door County Wisconsin, and others in the Chicago metropolitan area, illustrating that one does not have to travel to a distant wilderness to experience nature first hand.

Our work on this book began during a session at The Clearing in Ellison Bay. Parallel writing and artwork quickly became both dialogues with nature and with each other.

In the give and take of the creative process, sometimes the essay came first, sometimes the drawings. We had insights, gave mutual support. But always our intention has been to share our joint and individual quest for connection with nature and to show you a writer's shift in perspective and an artist's new vision from really looking.

And so we are making a genuine attempt to connect with you as well. We want you to come with us on this journey through ordinary experiences seen differently. Of course, telling or showing is not the same as a direct encounter with the wild. Our wish is that you, having read the essays and seen the drawings, will want to undertake your own voyage into the heart of nature, and find your own heart in the process.

CABIN FEVER

dialogues with nature

C. Kenney '92

C. Kenney '92

cormorants

*F*light of the Cormorants

> Out of North Bay,
> low over ruffled green waters,
> relentless as any Chinese army,
> piercing the yellow silk sky,
> squadron after squadron they came,
> echelon left,
> echelon right,
> wave upon wave,
> bold ink strokes scrawled
> across the dawn,
> cancelling summer.

Summer after summer I have come to this solitary stretch of Lake Michigan beach far away from the tourist's eyes and watched. Here I have learned to remain still, to listen from within as well as without, and to let the treasures seek me, let memories older than I drift in with the fog. I learned long ago the emptiness of racing from one point of beauty to another, camera in hand, snapping away, seeing nothing, missing everything.

Season after season I have come to know something of the rhythm of life on this wet edge of earth: the thrashing of carp in the shallow waters, spawning in the spring; busy, yellow-legged sandpipers moving like wind-up toys, dashing in stiff, erratic movements into the surf and back again with perfect timing; and the Arctic terns, their orange beaks canted down like electronic fish scopes, folding their wings in head-long kamikaze-like dives, smacking the water so hard it almost makes your head hurt watching, then going airborne again almost on the bounce, shaking water off their wings and twisting away from the envious ring-billed gulls, just a little demonstration on how to fly and how to

C. Kenney
11/93

fish for their lesser brothers. I have watched the red-breasted mergansers' comic head-bobbing courtship, seen their young practice tight-formation swimming against lurking predators, counted their diminishing numbers over the passing weeks and cheered on the survivors of summer.

The geese, the shore birds, gulls, terns, mallards, goldeneyes, and mergansers are the real residents here, and I am just a temporary visitor. Are they observing me as I observe them? Or am I regarded at all? Am I merely an intrusion who must be tolerated, something to be cautious of, or could I be part of a brotherhood? Could I qualify for belonging? What is required: an action, awareness, attitude, mindfulness, a vision? I come here each year with a hunger to be so much more than a bystander. I leave healed, but was not always satisfied that I belong. My quest was to become one with the scene, to know where I fit.

From out on the lake's far horizon there has always been a bird that has beckoned me, yet eluded me: the cormorant. One has to look hard to see that he is really out there, but once you know the subtleties, he can be spotted frequently. The cormorant is found at the seam of the lake shore's outer edge. Small black dots in long strings just above the surface of the water move in easy undulations just outside my range of easy knowing.

By mid-August, they are gathered by the hundreds, then thousands, forming into squadrons slowly swimming and flying southward, first sign of summer's ending. They float in great dark masses best seen with binoculars. Their movement is often from the rear forward. A group splashes down, swims along for a while, then the rear of the group appears to have decided they have gotten too far behind. They take off and fly over the main body, dragging others aloft as they go by, giving the appearance of pulling birds attached to a string. Landing at the front of the flotilla, they swim in the lead for a while until the whole procedure is repeated again by those now in the rear. All the while, new groups continuously fly in from the north and splash down at the end of the chain. A little later, the migration flights become less casual with much more flying and less swimming.

In this environment, the cormorant has always seemed shy and aloof, unlike the ones I have seen in Seattle and Key West posing on bollards right in front of waterfront restaurants' picture windows where they spread their wings out to dry in the sun and crane their snake-like necks. They have an ancient, reptilian look which makes it easy to imagine how such a bird might have evolved out of a sea serpent into a flying fisherman. Indeed, the cormorant is an accomplished swimmer and catches its prey under water, maneuvering with wings and propelling with its feet.

He seems almost better adapted for the water than the sky, for his aerodynamics are a little off, his body being oversized for the available wing. I have often wondered if this ratio of imbalance is a factor in the cormorants' preference for low-altitude flight, just skimming the water. Has he discovered the pilot's "ground effect," that slim zone between the surface and the wing which creates an additional buoyancy? Or is the cormorant merely a practical creature who doesn't care to exert the effort to fly very far from his source?

The Audubon Nature Encyclopedia provided some basic facts about my double-crested cormorant, but little about its essence. Obviously a big bird (thirty to thirty-five inches long), the cormorant with its long hooked beak, black feathers, and awkwardness on land is not known for its great beauty but for its superb fishing abilities. It is these very abilities that have helped reduce its once great numbers. Local newspaper accounts of their migrations down the Mississippi River flyway reported that they darkened the sky for hours, but that was in the last century. Enterprising Japanese took advantage of the birds' fishing ability to train them to do their fishing for them. Our fishermen, however, in a typical reaction to any competition from nature, slaughtered them by the thousands and destroyed nesting sites. Their numbers so dwindled during the fifties and sixties that they were put on the endangered

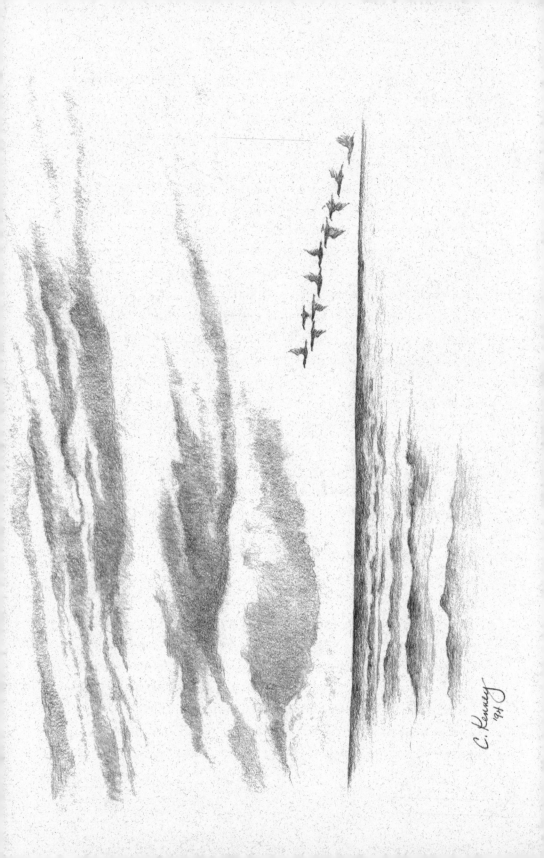

species list in Wisconsin. Also, research on the feeding habits of these birds indicated that their catch consisted largely of species of little commercial value, those which could crowd out the more valuable ones. The cormorant actually provided a service by keeping the less desirable fish populations in check.

Although still regarded as an enemy by fishermen because of the damage they sometimes do to fish trapped in the pond nets, the cormorant has been protected and is making a comeback. Spider Island lies three miles to the north and east of my shore and is now a National Wildlife Refuge. This island serves as a nesting ground for growing numbers of the gregarious cormorants. In the twenty years I have been watching, I have seen the vegetation disappear from the island with only the ghostly masts of dead cedars remaining on that thin, rocky shelf of limestone. The massive and rich droppings of so many birds have killed everything. While it would be illegal to visit the island, it would also be unpleasant for the senses. So, I am content to let the island remain a distant mystery, to not let my curiosity disturb the mass nesting, and spare myself the unpleasantness of great quantities of bird dung being cooked in the sun.

For so many years I considered myself fortunate to have witnessed the massing of the cormorants off this shore, a sight few eyes have seen. It is like knowing some special secret. Yet the cormorant eluded me, remained aloof. He would not come for scraps of bread like the ringbill gulls nor be drawn with curiosity about my dogs like the mergansers. He keeps his distance, remains completely a creature of the great lake, listens to his own calling and purpose. For me he became a symbol of something I could not quite put down in words, but he drew me to his far horizon. I had grown restless watching. Inside of me was a longing to know these birds in a different way from observing or reading about them. I wanted to experience them on a different, deeper level, to feel a touch of their mystery. My seasons of watching came to an end last year with the purchase of a sea-going kayak.

The August weather had been rotten, wet, and stormy. The main groups of cormorants appeared to have left two days before I got up my courage to launch. The wind had subsided, leaving long, green swells still dissipating their energy and fog banks breaking into patches. I convinced myself that it was either now or wait a whole year to try again. A few straggling groups of cormorants coming uncharacteristically close to shore because of the fog showed me the migration was not yet over. Perhaps they were still gathering in Moonlight Bay just to the south. Time to go.

The yellow needle nose of my kayak sliced easily through the crests, and the ocher lake bottom of limestone blocks looked like a submerged, but reassuring, highway I could walk back on in case of trouble. There is a wide, shallow shelf to Lake Michigan here, as the great Niagara Escarpment slowly emerges on a long incline, ending in its massive jutting jaw of cliffs on the west side of the peninsula. A quarter of a mile out, the bottom begins to fall away; at half a mile it can't be seen and at a mile the color of the water changes to the look of a deep green sea with a bottom beyond my knowing. The sense of my insignificance in this scene was complete. I was this tiny creature floating in an eggshell on the back of a moody, indifferent monster, one who could dispatch me with a flip of its tail. Patches of fog cut me off from the shore. I remembered, don't trust your senses, look for the clues: wind on your right cheek, you are headed out to open lake; wind on your left cheek, you are headed for shore; the waves are running northwest; the course for home lies forty-five degrees from the crests of the waves. Don't let confusion set in.

Breathe out fear, breathe in peace. Lighten the grip on the paddle. Allow yourself to be here. All is in order. Let this place be your place and not alien. Wait, listen, see, open all the senses. Remember why you came here. Be the humble apprentice. Prepare to learn. I floated, paddle across the gunnels, and listened to the wash of the waves, the only sound. My comfort zone had been left far behind, but a new kind of

heightened peace entered my body as I chose to accept the risks of being here and the risks of my very existence. I was vulnerable man afloat in the universe and trusting it.

How long I remained in that different state of awareness, I could not say. Without warning they burst upon me. Scores of black shapes came out of the fog headed straight for me. Calmly, at the last minute, they broke left and broke right or simply climbed a few feet to clear my head. I was in the center of this mass of black wings of soundless birds. There was no cry of alarm nor squawk of annoyance, just the soft whuff, whuff, whuff of great wings passing almost within reach of me. I turned south to run with them, shouting and whooping. More and more came all around me, and for a while, I had joined the migration, felt my blood surge, caught the exuberance of their movement, just a flicker of the spirit of a brotherhood of massed wings responding to the call of migration. Although they were faster than my best efforts, I never ran out of cormorants. It was the sound of breakers on the shoals of Marshall's Point out in the fog ahead of me that ended my run.

I brought my kayak about to run with the swells for a while, let them lift me from the stern, then slide on by in eerie, quiet motion. The troughs were deep. I was a long way out, a distance not measured in linear units. The last cormorant was swallowed by the fog as though there had never been any. It was just a moment, one I couldn't have photographed and perhaps don't even remember clearly; I just know I lived it full out. Putting the wave crests on my port side brought the wind to my left cheek and a heading for home shore.

There had been such an unreal quality to the experience that I wondered if it had ever happened. Was I really in a band of brothers; or just a crazy man out in the fog? In answer there floated in front of me one large dark feather. Yes! I had to have it. A trophy of the adventure! A symbol of acceptance! I charged the feather; it spun coyly away. I circled tightly, almost capsizing, and slipped the paddle under the feather; it floated off. Backing, turning, thrashing, cursing—that was not a dignified response to initiation. I had forgotten everything. Finally, my mind gentled, with an easy stroke I aligned myself and let the two of us drift together. I traveled home triumphant, cormorant feather in my headband.

C. Kenney
12/93

trash hawk

I am the raptor of the roadside, sweeping down County Highway ZZ. No vermin can rest on this sleepy road, for I am *Trash Hawk*, fierce and black! My white breast feathers spell *"Fate,"* the last thing they see before the swoop of wing and crush of talons. The kingbirds, redwings, and even kestrels flee their power-line perches and beagles bay at my approach, but they are not my prey, nor is the meadow vole, deer mouse, or least shrew. No nestling need be alarmed; my sensors are tuned not to the creatures of field or woods, but to the cast-offs of the four-wheeled two-leggeds.

My range runs down the stretch of road from Hazel Larson's place to the old Appleport School— no other challenges my territory.

Before my metamorphosis, I was a runner of these country roads. I ran against other men for the gold, the silver, or the bronze. I ran against the abstraction of time, until time and my body taught me the empty folly of competition, a hunger never sated, a hunger that devours its own host.

Then I ran for the beauty of an undulating ribbon of road where daisies and Queen Anne's lace swayed and cheered me on, and blue-eyed chicory watched me pass, where old Joe Pye weed stood tall in the wet culvert nodding approval, where meadows sweet with rain waved perfumed handkerchiefs in my face, where bluebirds and goldfinches splashed color across my path like tiny bobbins darting through the loom, where meadowlarks trilled and bob-o-links called from fence posts.

Then I saw beauty spoiled by the careless toss of an empty can, and another, and another. My rage inflamed me. Changed me. I began to snatch up cans, crush them. Carry them off. My appetite grew and grew. First from a can or two, then bottles. Wrappers. Plastic. Papers. Rags. Hubcaps. Trim. All became grist for my craw. I became this voracious, black-feathered *thing*. Talons grew from my fingernails, wings extended from my arms. I became *Trash Hawk*.

Nothing could escape my raptor's eye, no green beer bottle hiding in the tall grass, no film of polypropylene trying to look like a spiderweb covered with dew, not even the tiny Brach's wrapper foiled by the sun. The bones of this roadside were picked clean when I was done.

I heard from nowhere the voice of old Kate Smith singing "God bless America, land that I love," and I sang along in a new version of "God help America, land that I love, she's been trashed from sea to shining sea, from her clear-cut mountains to her prairies made a memory, to her oceans white with styrofoam; God help America, my home sweet home."

My mentor, the marsh hawk, circled the cabin one day, sent a single dark feather spiraling down, inspiring me on. My brother, the crow, who handles the road kill, acknowledged my work, left me three black feathers at the end of a three-bag day.

So out on County Double Z there's a man in a black running suit with a black feather in his sweatband, carrying a black trash bag, looking like some macabre, out-of-season Santa who thinks he's a damn bird!

But, beware! He's making a list of who's naughty and not nice. And, without a fast-food joint within miles, it's the beer drinkers and cigarette smokers hands down. Surprised? Why? They'll always be the last to "get it."

"Ain't it a shame what them tourists do," says Mabel Carlson as she sees Trash Hawk haulin' a heavy load. Well, I got news for you, old girl: it ain't just the tourists spreading styrofoam over the land. It's the local teenies with their weenie brains enrolled in prep school for AA, dumping the evidence, cans, cases and all, before good Sheriff Gottcha can make a collar.

And, it ain't the folks from the North Shore of Chicago flippin' out all those Skoal tobacco cans at Three Springs. It's some yokel in a pickup who ain't grow'd up yet. Sure, I admit, a man's gotta chew what a man's gotta chew, but we don't need to know about it.

C. Kenney '92

It's those tall-in-the-saddle Marlboro "men" and ultimate-stud Camel smokers still sucking on their mother's breast and expecting her to clean up after 'em. Of course, real men don't give a damn about the in-virmint or pole-ution and that kind of stuff, but do us a favor, fellas, keep it to yourselves. Next time you light up, drop a plastic bag over your head.

Like I say, the evidence is in—you know who you are and so does Trash Hawk. In the next lifetime, he's coming back as a pterodactyl or even more fearsome beast with a taste for tainted human flesh. Then beware, you motorized swine, because you're gonna be mine, all mine!

tracking a new
deer legend

*T*here was just enough snow to make cross-county skiing a reasonable possibility; even so, the little scales on the bottoms of my skis would sing-out now and then as they skimmed the bare places or went over an uncovered branch. The Skokie Lagoons were looped with curving trails following the bends of their shores where early skiers had grabbed the advantage of the morning's snow. Main paths never appealed much to me, so I veered off at the first bend.

The sun was just beginning to slide below the February horizon when I left the well-worn trail of others and headed into the deeper woods. I was not seeking human contact; in fact, I was trying to avoid it. The contact I wanted was of a different kind. It was with nature itself. Here, in this scruffy patch of woods, on this thin island washed on one side by the heavy traffic of Edens Expressway and blockaded on the other by expensive homes, a variety of wildlife had been able to make a stand. I wanted to encounter them firsthand to see what they might teach me, believing, as the first Americans believed, that they are messengers and that they still hold the thin threads of connection between ourselves and the world we have denied.

It was the deer I sought this time, those delicate, beguiling, troublesome creatures who were creating so many conflicting emotions and controversies. I followed a single deer track northward into the thickening woods, ducking nasty buckthorn branches which snatched at my cap and grabbed for my scarf. The scene was a black and white etching with the snow reflecting just enough of the remaining light to give a slight tint to the land and illuminate my way. The woods took on a savanna-like character that allowed easier passage, and the larger oaks defined a subtle corridor. Another set of tracks merged with the first. Others could be seen nearby running parallel courses through the trees. More convergence of tracks, and still more, like the coming together of railroad lines might be seen from the air as they gather in some great terminus. Yes, here is where the deer were yarding-up. I moved more slowly now, being careful not to snap twigs, and searched for shapes which would seem out of place.

There was slight movement ahead and to my left. I froze and scanned. Two hundred feet away a doe raised her head from browsing, looked around, and then lowered it again. I inched ahead, holding my breath, stopping whenever she did, and closed to within less than a hundred feet. Then other shapes emerged from behind her on a slight rise: two, three, four and more, nine in all. Too many for such a small woods. Since I was downwind, they did not pick up my scent, yet they seemed to sense my presence. One by one, they all raised their heads. I just watched and didn't even twitch.

The one closest to me stared in my direction and, as with a silent signal, told the others where I was.

There we stood in the chill stillness of February twilight watching one another with a penetrating intensity. I was detailing the perfection of their winter uniforms. They were trying to determine who I was and what my intentions were. No sound. No scent. No movement. Nine pairs of alert ears defined by neat tan linings were stretched taut and quivering, pointed at me like radar scopes trying to pick up a bogey. I was being held by nine pairs of eyes, locked on for identification. Now, we had contact, but would there be "connection"?

To merely see wildlife in a highly urbanized area is both a gift and a reminder of what is missing in us. But we have been separated so long that something deep within us has been forgotten. We have been impoverished at the soul level. We do not even know of our loss, though we sometimes feel a surge of energy and excitement at a sighting of some animal without understanding where that feeling comes from. Occasionally the rescue of a wounded bird or small forest creature becomes the most emotionally important thing in our lives, yet we do not comprehend that we are feeding an ancient hunger to reunite, to re-establish the intimate connections we once had but have renounced in our hell-bent conquest of nature.

I struggled against all my hurry-up notions, the get-on-with-it, move-ahead instincts conditioned by urban living that would have had me press on and scatter the herd like a small boy casting a stone into the unrippled pond just to see it splash. We hurry into movement and action so we do not have to contemplate the deeper stillness of things that terrifies us so. Something made me stop, made me relax and let go of every thought, to unclench my teeth, drop my shoulders, and, at last, remember to breathe. Somehow I caught that this was not an ordinary occurrence, though I might have made it one in my surface ignorance. All that existed was the moment and the connection it brought. Their eyes and mine looking into the center of one another. Our breaths rose and fell together, steamed upward as smoke might from a pipe that passed the circle. All those soft faces defined by three dark pieces of charcoal for a nose and a pair of eyes engaging my own for long, long minutes. I shivered, but not from the cold. I felt the simple power of the event, but did not know what to do about it. As if there were something to "do."

How long we stood motionless there, I couldn't say. My eyes went from face to face and back again. All said the same.

It was a time for me to be still, to listen deeply beyond my own hearing, a time for allowing thoughts not of my own. A deepening state filled everything in that shallow swale: the deer, my body, the snow, even the fallen trees and young saplings. It was as though we had assembled at a sacred place to exchange an understanding. What it was I couldn't say. What was I supposed to "get"? I thought of how the scientist and the professional wildlife "managers" would scoff in their arrogance at my naive questioning, but I let that thought go. I returned to the unrelenting, patient eyes. Still no answer.

At last, I purposefully raised my ski pole like a baton. In unison, like a well-trained chorus line, they spun on cue and left the stage waving their white-fringed behinds. The darkness of the woods absorbed them. I remained for a few moments to let the images sink in and to allow myself to acknowledge what a fortunate man I was. On my way out of the woods as the light drained away, so did the ecstasy of the moment. I was filled with an overpowering sadness about the ultimate fate of these beautiful, gentle creatures which we have revered so long. There were too many in this small place, too many in all of our forest preserves and conservation areas. The nine healthy does, mixed with a single, able buck, will each produce a pair of spotted twins in the spring, if the winter is not too severe. This small herd could leap from ten to twenty-eight in a single season.

Why is this happening? On one level the answers are straightforward, although not simple. The deer's natural enemies vanished over a century ago under the sentence of "vermin." Hunting is prohibited in these urban woods surrounded by well-to-do suburban developments, and the only predator is the automobile. Also, their habitat is shrinking as we farm more and more available land and develop attractive wooded sites. Without restraint on their population growth the small herd I encountered and scores more will explode geometrically in these precious woods and devastate them. Their numbers will move through the woods like an army of mechanized landscapers in a subdivision, mowing and trimming everything in sight. They will leave browse lines on the trees as though some overzealous gardener had lost control and pruned the whole woods.

Eventually, there will not be enough food in the forest preserves to feed this unchecked population surge. The deer are already moving into the yards and gardens of the upper-middle-class homes where enchanted owners once hand-fed "Bambi" and were thrilled to have deer as neighbors. They will watch in horror the destruction of their expensive landscaping by the starving deer. Stewards of the nature preserves, volunteers and restorationists, all passionate supporters of wildlife, are beginning to grumble about "forest cows" and "hoofed rats" as they see their precious, laboriously restored, woodland eradicated overnight. These gentle people confronted with the "deer problem" begin to mutter murder under their breath and then feel guilty. The cry, "kill Bambi" rises up. "Hire sharpshooters! Thin the herd, but please don't let me see it!"

Perhaps the "why" of it all goes beyond our everyday answers. I wondered about all that as I left the woods, brushed off my skis, and loaded them in the van. Sitting there in the dark, I suddenly recalled that stirring quote from Aldo Leopold's *A Sand County Almanac* in a passage titled, "Thinking Like a Mountain." He speaks of the deer "dying of their own too much" as a result of our eliminating their natural enemies, and how a mountain can come to fear the deer as much as the deer fear the wolf, for it can be browsed to death. There was something haunting in Leopold's phrase, "dying of their own too much," and it kept playing over and over in my head.

I wondered what the ancient ones would say about our "deer problem." What would all this look like from a spiritual perspective instead of from our narrow human experience? What was the deeper "why" that was eluding me? What was the significance of this current man-deer relationship? What was that relationship once before, long ago when we were aware of our interconnections? The Native Americans communicated with wildlife in ways we never bothered to learn. They developed myths and legends which gave meaning to the bonds between man and all other forms of life. This was especially true for the life-giving, life-sustaining animals such as the deer and the buffalo. These animals supplied the basics of food, clothing, and shelter. The relationship was both intimate and violent, but it had meaning, and the killing was not for sport.

The ancient ones prayed for the soul of the animal they must kill to ensure its return. They killed with respect and ceremony. There was covenant between the respectful hunter and the hunted. They were linked in an endless circle of life, death, and renewal. There was no separation, and man learned many lessons from the animals. The white man broke the circle with his thoughtless slaughter. He would kill and

kill, without need, without ceremony or respect. The white man was, and is, ignorant of his linkages to all of life. But what of the four-leggeds? Have they forgotten the covenant or forsaken it, or are they still honoring it and willing to teach us when we are ready to learn?

I thought, if I were an ancient one returned to tell the story, what new legend would I speak of? The deer no longer comes to the hunter to provide his food, clothing, and shelter. The deer come to starve in our faces. The deer come to us to demonstrate our peril with their own lives, a fate we refuse to see. They come to warn us with their plight that we are the ones who are going to "die of our own too much." We are consuming, destroying, and poisoning our own small habitat with our own exploding numbers.

Mentally, we have created a separation between ourselves and the earth as our source. We spend its wealth lavishly without concern for the balance sheet. We live in the illusory bubble of our marvelous technology and cling to the false belief that somehow science will save us from the final accounts due in full. If we fail to recognize and heal our deep addictions to ever higher levels of consumption, then, in spite of our apparent wealth and security, we will create our own Bangladesh or Somalia. That was the message of the deer. That is the legend I would tell if I were an ancient one returned to interpret the deer.

C. Kenney
'94

the healing river

*A*rriving home that October afternoon, I was anticipating my first direct contact with people after having been so remote from them. As I approached my house, I became aware of how much I was smiling, how my body floated across the landscape, barely touching the ground. Never had I felt so light, so free. I thought I might have to be tethered to remain grounded. This lightness of being did not come from the joy of reuniting with my family, however. What I was experiencing were the effects of a powerful "medicine," as the ancient ones might call it. No meditation, massage, Jacuzi, or steam bath could have had such restorative power as that earlier experience of the day.

I had not returned from some far-off retreat, but from a location less than an hour away from my city home; not from a whole season of wilderness wanderings, but from a journey of a few hours; not from some vast territory, but from the smallest of overlooked realms. It had been an adventure of the body, mind, and spirit within the narrowest of physical limits. For a brief moment, I had been able to step out of the insulating capsule of my artificial existence of living on the earth unmindful of its all powerful influence on my life. Being reintroduced to the "river" of my life put me back in touch with the very core of being, the core too long ignored. I had been shown how much modern man had lost and how much he suffers, unknowingly, from not being in a state of grace with nature. The miracle came in the reawakening of memories of wildness, a sensory recall of another time of living closer to the earth as an ancient man.

The mechanics and the geography of this profound voyage were really quite simple. I took a kayak trip on the upper Des Plaines River in late October.

Just "where" is this river, or what is the where of it? The Des Plaines River begins just north across the Wisconsin border as a small stream meandering through a township named "Pleasant Prairie" — and indeed it must have been once, very long ago. Ultimately, the Des

Plaines connects with the Illinois and the Mississippi and goes all the way to the Gulf of Mexico.

My experience with the river this day was within just a short segment. This section of the river lies in a flat, shallow valley about half a mile wide, part of a series of swales and ridges paralleling the shore of Lake Michigan and marking pauses in the retreat of the last glacier. At the valley's borders, the land rises quickly to the breathtaking height of thirty-five feet along the crests of the moraines that set the river's course. Living in an old glacial landscape, one must be attuned to subtleties or see nothing at all. A tree line of oaks marks the tops of the morainal ridges, but there is a wholly different vegetational landscape in the grassy, wet valley.

The section of the river I traveled was further defined by manmade features, a pair of bridges: Rosencrans Road on the north and Wadsworth Road on the south. They were my only markers along this water trail. At the outer limits, the river valley is contained between two manmade features: Highway 41, taking the first high ground to the west, and the Chicago, Milwaukee, St. Paul, and Pacific Railroad embankment to the east. Their alignment shows a grudging deviation from a preference for straight-line courses. The highway and railroad follow long, easy engineer's curves only where necessary to keep their feet dry and appease the wet valley. How strong the desire must have been to channel the river's wandering into a nice straight ditch. This errant river moves in its own capricious dance between rigid neighbors, brushing a shoulder against one and then the other, turning back upon itself, then striking out again more or less south. The river has its own special wisdom and mission. It is in no rush to leave for destinations downstream.

I can use all the proper manmade references, tell you the roads that cross or parallel its course, pin down its location as running through sections 15, 22, and 27 of township 46 north, range 22 east of Newport township. Looking over a United States Geological Survey map and see-

ing the long valley and its river defined by such place names tells me precisely where I am, but does it really? Location, yes. Realm, no.

The Des Plaines River, like so many others in our country, has been greatly abused or "degraded," as the ecologists would say. Sections have been dredged and channelized; its watershed has been cleared, farmed, mined, developed, and paved over; pollutants of all kinds have drained into it from the surrounding lands; and sedimentation from soil erosion has washed into its channel. All of this, plus the introduction of alien plant species, has drastically altered the life and character of the river. Yet, one can sense that the "spirit" of the river is not dead and could be revived if the worst abuses were halted. Experiments on working with the river and its wetlands are actually being carried out by Wetlands, Inc., just south of the section I traveled.

For months I had wanted to explore the river, but each time I checked the water level at the canoe landing off Wadsworth Road, there was more mud than water. Inevitably, I had to settle for a trail hike instead. While the woodlands, savannas, and open prairies had their charm, I was seeking the water, and it kept eluding me. The river would reveal itself only for a short stretch before slipping around a gentle bend and wandering off to hide in its broad floodplain obscured by thick willow shrubs, tall reeds, grasses, and sedges. But, this time, recent rains had brought a rise in water level. Standing on the timbered decking of the launch area and looking down at the river, I could see a definite current. Along the bank, recently flooded smartweed was colored mud-gray. The river was dropping again. Today was the day, and now was the time. Any delay of a day or two might make the journey a frustrating one of getting stuck in too many shallows.

Another kayaker, remembering the rains of last week, had come to test the river. He had a rugged, well-seasoned craft made of wood, one he had built himself for wilderness journeys in Canada. He wanted to compare crafts, swap stories, and share enthusiasm for kayaking. Nice fella, but human companionship was not what I was seeking. Not today. Quite the opposite. Later, perhaps. Over a beer at the near-by tavern called "The Shanty" overlooking the wetlands. Maybe, but not now. I was seeking solitude. Nodding, smiling, and giving one syllable answers, I kept moving.

I asked him which way he was headed. "South with the current," he said.

Good, I thought. "I'm going upstream first, then coast back. Maybe I'll see you later." As I got ready to launch, I gave him a big grin and friendly wave, more from relief than cordiality.

I slid the kayak down the steep gravel slope anchored by red dogwood and staghorn sumac and took great pains not to get wet as I boarded. I was not ready for complete intimacy with this murky river. There is a feeling of instant joy that comes with launch. My reaction is involuntary and always catches me by surprise. The smooth, swift cut of the kayak through the water, powered by my own arms, always brings a sensation of fresh discovery. A sigh of deep peace accompanies those first few strokes, and a smile slides into place as standard equipment.

The first landmark, the large concrete bridge carrying Wadsworth Road over the river, lay immediately ahead. The bridge was accompanied by a monstrous power line, not the most appealing view for beginning a journey into nature. There was an old rusted muffler and tail pipe projecting from the mud under the bridge, just a little tribute from the highway, a classic symbol of our attitude towards rivers. The current had slowed in its passage around the supporting pillars, causing the river to drop some of its sediment and leaving a muddy shallow hard to navigate. I had to dig my paddle into the muck and shove the kayak along. Was this stretch going to be typical of what I would experience? Breaking free into deeper waters, the river took me briefly west and parallel to the road. I could hear the morning rush-hour traffic crossing the bridge.

There was an odd moment of self-consciousness as I wondered what those motorists might think about this guy in a bright yellow kayak on a workday morning navigating this cloudy little stream. "Is he nuts? How come he gets to do that and I gotta work?" Or maybe, "God he's lucky, I wish I could." Probably only a few felt any envy, and of those, an even smaller number would ever really consider acting on the desire to actually get out on the river. Why? Why have we all retreated so far from personal contact with the earth when it can refresh our arid spirits? I have looked for the answers in myself. Fear? Inertia? The trance state of separation our collective culture has imposed upon us?

It is not easy to break free of the accumulated layers of comfort and the numbness we have wrapped around ourselves. We may still be afraid to touch the earth at any deep level and let our aliveness resonate with it. I made no judgments about the frantic motorists. I was like them. But for me, it had become clear that my survival demanded breaking free of those mechanical currents which were carrying my life to unwanted destinations. My thoughts shifted back to the river itself. There was that nostalgic scent of fresh river mud drying in the sun that reminded me of my own Huck Finn days on the old Ohio River so long ago. My urban world dissolved behind me. There was just the river, me, and my craft. The river held my gaze, took me away. I never looked back.

A little turn to the north put the world to my back and opened up a broad, sinuous stretch of water reflecting the green and yellow of willows turning with the fall and a perfect blue sky, all cut and fit with the neatness of a stained-glass window. No wind. No sound. A cathedral filled with the hush of holiness, the kind of place that makes you want to remove your hat and shoes, speak in soft whispers, if you speak at all. Was it really okay to be here? Yes, but I must show respect. Still, I was only in the outer chamber, and as I approached the large sanctuary of open sky and water, my path was barred by a snag that went from shore to shore. It was a large, fallen willow now almost completely submerged and acting as a low dam, collecting debris and allowing a thin sheet of water to pass over its prone trunk. Perhaps a hardy run against

C. Kenney '92

this obstacle would carry me over the threshold. My energetic strokes got me exactly halfway, stuck atop the log. I had hoped to avoid physical contact with the river, but it would have none of that. In an awkward, slippery exit, I planted my feet on the river bottom. My aqua socks immediately received a deposit of river muck and grit. Now the toll had been paid, we had been properly introduced, and the journey could continue. I had to laugh at my pretentiousness. How could I truly experience this river without becoming part of it? I might as well have stayed in my car as to have remained sanitized and separated, safe within my little plastic shell.

Once across the willow dam, I entered the inner world of the river with all its subtle little variations of forms on display. The channel broadened; quiet pools of waterlilies were tucked in close to the shore, the natural levee was marked by lines of shaggy, unkempt willows, their branches shooting off askew in all directions. The river course became a willow world. All along its path were willow trees, willow shrubs, willow dams and snags, young willows, great-grandfather willows, tipped willows, and, most handsome of all, low willow bridges arching over the river, showing off nature's deeply grooved, "hand-carved" beams.

A great blue heron a hundred yards upstream unfolded his giant wings and lazily launched himself in search of a perch beyond my view. I invaded his privacy over and over again, but it could not be helped. We engaged in a stalking game of hide and seek to see if I could spot him before he flew. I lost every time.

Beyond the willow picket marking the stream bank was the broad, treeless floodplain filled with sedges and grasses. Each slight shift in the rise of land was marked by nature's own response in plant life. These riverside companions showed a strong sense of order, a plan as well as beauty. The bright October sun brought out all the distinctions in color in that tawny fall landscape: the blonds, the russets, the tans, the burgundies and grays, as well as shades between. These colors stacked themselves along the riverbank in long, parallel bands, marking subtle changes in elevation. As the land started to climb at the outer limits of the flood plain, cottonwoods took the first high ground, followed by oaks on the upper slopes. The oaks still clung to their leaves, marking a high green border following the river at a respectful distance.

The river began to wander in long languid loops as though uncertain where to go in its quest for the sea in this flat valley. But, the river is wise and knows better that we its mission. I was grateful for the absence of the Army Corps of Engineers and their passion for dredging, straightening, and clearing to maintain an eight-foot channel for navigation as on the Ohio River I knew as a boy. I welcomed the snags and the wild look of it all. I was thankful that no landscaper had plucked the brow of the river, planted grass on its shore, or tidied up the trees.

Around each curve to the next new stretch were variations on a theme, small surprises to delight the eye with shifts in lighting, color, and the arrangement of landscape responses. Going from broad sunlit stretches to narrow channels shaded by willows, to slip under a low willow bridge into an enclosed world of shadow sprinkled with light filtering through the narrow leaves, made my journey one of unfolding joy.

My paddle broke the reflecting mirror with only a gurgle. The yellow nose of the kayak kept pointing to the next bend, the next little chamber of surprises. The rhythmic sway of my arms with easy strokes was in keeping with the serenity of the scene. This was no race, no workout; there was no urgent destination. I was already where I wanted to be. There was only the idle thumbing through pages of wonder, watching light passing through a prism of color as seen in the slow scan from bank to bank. There was time to allow the different forms to be let into my mind, feelings about them register. Familiar plants were recognized as friends without the urge to botanize or classify the many species which composed the colonies so pleasing to the eye, not in this moment. There was only a soaking up of the shapes and colors to replenish the spirit. Here was the opportunity for indulging the child-

C. Kenney
'93

like giddiness of my good fortune to be in this time and place. It was a time to take note without taking notes, to appreciate, not analyze. I knew enough of what was going on around me to fit the pieces into my left brain and to keep it occupied. This was a voyage for the other hemisphere of the brain. It became the right brain's trip to the candy store! Bend around bend, the kid in me kept saying, "Wow! Look at that!" This voyage became a journey outside of time, outside of the frantic obsessions of urban living. There were no people hurrying to be somewhere else, no automobiles, no mechanical sounds, no houses, not even a farm or a stalk of corn. There was just the stream, its family, and me. There was not so much as a cheery canoe with occupants to wave a friendly greeting. I was grateful. Another human face would have disrupted the dream, broken the ephemeral connection between me and my new community, reminding me that I was only in a narrow seam of nature, briefly hidden from my greater world which had gone all wrong.

So I clung to my illusion of wildness and focused on the small details of stream life: the gray high-water marks that recent floods had left on stream-bank shrubs; the wonderful bank-cutting curves of meanders; the furrowed bark of an ancient black willow tree; the feel of the current pushing against my shins as I slid my kayak over a slick willow dam; the composition of stones in the exposed streambank as it cut into a moraine topped by a black oak; and the grace of the current as it curved around the big, erratic boulders dumped by the last glacial bulldozer.

Only one portage was required. That was around a huge willow tipped into the stream and blocking all passage, over or under. There was a deep U shape in the tall grasses and sedges marking the path of others before me and a rounded depression where deer had spent the night. Later, I found my body had picked up two unwanted passengers at this point—a pair of the dreaded deer ticks. Seeing the portage path in the grass reminded me that I might soon be coming to the Rosencrans Road bridge, and I did not want the illusion to end so soon. It was time to head back. "Time," that word again—as hard to shake as the sight of my fellow man. "Time," an explosion in the world of tranquility, a barbarian in the state of "being."

Saving my curiosity as to what might be around the next bend for another trip, I brought the yellow bow about in a hard turn downstream. Although there had been no sense of laboring against the current on the way up, the acceleration of the kayak, once we had reversed course, sent a tingle through my body. This segment of the trip was going to be effortless fun. I could either stroke to build up speed or just do a little token paddling and let the current do all the work. No effort or struggle to make it back—just like a ride in the tunnel of love at Riverview Park, except the light was better and there were no female distractions.

While each gracefully curving meander was familiar, it was seen in a fresh perspective, a different blend of shadow and light filtered through the leaves. Big splashes of sun alternated with murky canyons of massive willow trunks. There was muskrat mud for bank dens, lily launching pads for frogs, cattail perches for redwings (and maybe a yellow-headed blackbird). A swift, carving current had left a high bank for swallows, and sluggish, shallow pools had been arranged for that lanky spearfisherman, the great blue heron. Sets prepared for nature's great magic kingdom show could be found around each bend. I was getting a private tour arranged just for me. Quiet, off-season, not open to the public, most of the entertainers gone, but what a show it was going to be next spring!

I lazily played the current through the meanders, ruddering to the deeper outside of the curves where the river accelerated. I could feel the grace and perfection while watching the marvel of the river's work. There were even a few gentle rapids formed by those "cannonballs" of basalt casually dropped by the last glacier. My long craft was better designed for riding the rollers of Lake Michigan than for negotiating tight turns between boulders in a narrow channel, but I just played

C. Kenney
'94

C. Kenney 6/93

bumper boat and laughed my way through them. Sometimes we would scrape bottom and almost run aground, but a fresh surge of current would heft us free and we would head for deeper water. The aluminum rudder would "clank, clank, clank" on the bouldered bottom with decreasing frequency like a leadsman taking soundings from the deck of an old paddle boat. When we cleared the shallows at last, I sang out, "Mark twain!" and we would sail around the next bend in the good, deep, swift current. Then, I would lean back, put my cheek up against the late October sun, and just toe the rudders to stay centered in the current. Not a bad way to live one's life: find its natural flow, stay centered in its current, and keep your face to the light.

Here and there, I sized up a protected rise in the land, a natural levee, and speculated on its potential as a primitive campsite for the night. Who would know? This wetland was inaccessible except by canoe or kayak. Prohibited, no doubt. So? When did the regulations ever stop you if you thought you could twist the tail of the bureaucrats? The truth was, I was searching for a way to remain, a way to extend these few hours of "island" experience, knowing that the next bend of the river might reveal the last stretch to journey's end. It wasn't the regulations that made me let go of the fantasy and continue to drift on. It was those two deer ticks I picked out of my bare thigh that sobered me. A promised return for the February thaw to do a little Eskimo kayaking brightened me. Even knowing I couldn't carry the true essence of this voyage with me, I could remember enough to want to seek the river again.

Re-entering the last open stretch where the river broadens, slows, and becomes one with the marsh and wet prairie, I also stalled, drifted, and put no effort in moving forward. "Go slowly, slowly," a voice said. "Take time to admire the construction of the beaver lodge projecting its chiseled, pencil-point branches. Let lily pads catch your craft, slow your return. Give the wary heron no reason to launch."

The blast of the Amtrak train's whistle blowing for the Wadsworth crossing brought me back. Overhead, a small plane purred by at low altitude on its final approach to Waukegan Airport. Soon I could see the high-tension wires and the Wadsworth Road bridge. I fly planes, ride on trains, and drive cars, but they were alien intrusions on the peace I had come to know in the past few hours. Only the promise I made to myself to return gave me the resolve to haul my kayak up the bank and lash it to the top of my van.

At home that evening, I glanced again at the U.S.G.S. quadrangle named "Wadsworth" and the thin wriggle of blue called the Des Plaines River. What this random blue ribbon truly represented was a chance to briefly escape a rigid, linear world, the mindless pursuit of unfulfilling goals, and reconnect with true source. That such an opportunity can still be found in this conquered land is a miracle in itself. We don't have to hurl ourselves on a jet all the way to the West to some grand wilderness in order to find what we have lost, what we still need. The whistle of the Amtrak train at the Wadsworth crossing reminded me that even Thoreau didn't have to go so far from civilization to know more of the peace of solitude and nature. The Fitchberg Railroad rattled by, touching the end of Walden Pond about 100 rods from where he dwelled. If we are willing, open and patient, we can still find our connection to the earth in some of the most unlikely places. We can astound ourselves at how quickly the healing will begin.

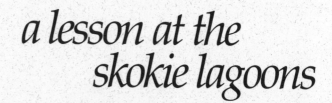

a lesson at the
  skokie lagoons

*A*fter a season of challenging the Lake Michigan swells in my kayak, I was looking forward to some quiet, meditative time on a small, manmade body of water known as the Skokie Lagoons. Previously, my only acquaintance with this recreational area had been in winter when I sought out the beauty and tranquility of its woods and frozen ponds on my cross-country skis. Now, in this seam between fall and winter was my chance to learn a new face of an old setting, to put myself in the path of unknown experiences.

I arrived in the nearly empty parking lot just off Lake Avenue on a quiet weekday, my yellow kayak looking like a large banana strapped to the top of my van. There were a few good old boys in plaid shirts and some swarthy ethnics scattered along the shore with fishing poles, but no one on the water. Dragging my craft across the short green grass to the water's edge, I stopped abruptly and almost changed my mind. Clinging to the muddy lip of the shoreline was a most foul-looking film of brown and green scum. In this net was suspended debris of plastic, bottles, and papers, small tokens of appreciation left by the recreationists who love this place so much.

Boarding my kayak took extra measures of care to prevent making contact with any part of that disgusting fluid. Please! Not a splash! Not a drop! A capsize would bring thoughts of hepatitis, not drowning. Successfully launched, I continued to paddle lightly, cautiously, as though trying to allow as little contact between my craft and the water as possible, tip-toeing across the lagoon. Farther out from the shore, the quality of the water "improved" somewhat; at least we had left the scum and debris behind. Still, the water was a turbid brown-green and thick with suspended sediment. I began to speculate as to whether the bottom of my hull might not dissolve out from under me before my journey was complete.

As I was moving out to the center of the lagoon, one of the ethnics started shouting at me and waving his arms. Was I in danger? Had

I committed some violation of fishing ethics? He was as incomprehensible as he was distressed. Eventually his arm waving translated into some pointing at the water, and I noticed a long, thin, black object moving in my direction. It was an unattached fishing pole swimming out towards me. Unattached, that is, on the fisherman end.

Maneuvering to intercept, I paddled back toward shore and snagged the runaway pole, but felt the line go slack when we hit the shallows. The man's smile fell away to sadness when he lifted the empty line. Still, he was grateful to have his fishing pole returned. In a heavy, broken accent he explained apologetically that his wife was not an accomplished fisherman, had gotten excited, and dropped the pole. I said I was sorry about his fish, but figured that losing it may have added at least several months to their lives, if not years.

Resuming my journey, I was already convinced that this would not be an aesthetic adventure with nature. What moment of beauty could be captured here, what lesson could be learned in this degraded place? Some aggressive stroking took me around the bend of the center island and out of the view of the fishermen. Small splashes from my paddle began to dry into gray-green blobs on my bare legs, reminding me to slow down; besides, one can see or learn little charging into a scene. Did I want exercise or knowledge?

Placing the paddle across the gunnels, I let my momentum drift me into the next scene as I let my breath go, quieted my mind, became open and receptive to whatever might present itself. I tried to imagine myself as an explorer far from the works of man and seeing this place for the first time. Signs of early fall splashed a yellow tint over the wall of green flanking the edges of the river, and individual leaves floating by were large-beamed vessels, their stems erect like empty masts. Cottonwood, willow, maple, poplar, and elm formed a regatta identifying their hosts of the shore.

Great, twisted and contorted forms of fallen trees lined the banks of the island, their dead roots and branches seeming like resident sculp-

tures of some museum of modern art. Kingfishers took good advantage of these high, clear perches, but what they could see in these waters was beyond me.

Black ducks burst out from the cover of flood-downed trees, their leafy green crowns still intact. Bursting thistles hanging over the bank launched whole divisions of chutists who landed lightly on the water. The imperceptible puffs of wind sent them cartwheeling across the glassy surface.

Then my quiet patience brought me the prize I had been waiting for, the one my haste would have cost me, the one I could not have seen. While I sat in contemplative silence, barely drifting, the shape of the crooked neck of a great blue heron emerged from among the distorted dead branches of a fallen cottonwood right in front of me. Slowly I dropped my hands to my weapon, a large-bore Canon, and raised it up to firing position. Holding my breath, I pushed the shutter release and was shocked at how loud it sounded. The heron remained on his perch, so I continued to fire away while drifting closer. At my slow approach, his distance tolerance seemed to be about twenty-five yards; then he unfolded his great wings, flexed into the air, and, with that casualness characteristic of his flight, paddled easily away around the next bend.

The game was on. I knew he would not be far around the bend, on some new perch and blended into the landscape. Could I spot him and take another shot before stumbling across his perimeter and launching him into flight? For the moment, all revulsion to the degradation of the place left me, and I became caught up in the game of hide and seek with the heron. Often I would spot him out of camera range and have to drift ever so slowly toward him while he struck classic poses, seemingly taunting me. Once I flushed him without ever seeing him before he flew. My focus of complete attention upon this magnificent bird and our little game was like a gift from nature, teaching me once again how healing is the unity of our connection. But it was not the last lesson.

I decided to follow my prize around one more bend, then leave him in peace. This time he allowed me a little closer, probably because he was fishing. He would cast one seemingly wary and disdainful eye at me, then contemplate the muddy waters before him. He struck almost too quickly to see, brought up a small fish, put it away and flew off. I thanked him for the demonstration and headed back to my launch spot.

Maybe this place is not so bad after all. I had been able to lose myself in nature for a time in spite of my initial reaction. Maybe this is as good as we can do in such a highly urbanized area. Maybe this is what we settle for. Still, with the heron gone, I began to notice the styrofoam cups and bottles caught in the beautiful network of exposed roots along the bank. And, as I rounded the bend closest to Edens Highway, the noise of the traffic began to drown out the song of the cicadas. If I had had company, I would have had to raise my voice to be heard.

With quick strokes I put that segment behind me, then began to coast home. From over my left shoulder, the one closest to the island, came an unfamiliar sound. My first glance revealed nothing. Again the sound, like a snort. Turning and looking back this time, I saw a young buck whitetail watching me, following me. He would take a few steps, then, stiff-legged, plant his front feet and snort at me. In retrospect, I could be amused and flattered that he might have seen me as a potential challenge to his harem rights with the does, but that was not my first thought. In listening with a different ear, what came to me in a flash was, "Damn you! How dare you! Damn you!"

I make no apologies about anthropormorphism, to science, or to the practical mind. I don't talk to animals, and, as far as I know, they don't speak to me. Yet, I do know there are messages and symbols constantly being broadcast just on the boundaries of our awareness and beyond our ability to completely comprehend. To me, this message was clear, even though it came through common deer behavior. My immediate reaction was a combination of guilt, embarrassment, and apology. "I'm sorry. No, it wasn't me. You don't understand. Yes, my kind perhaps,

C. Kenney
11/93

but not me. My culture, certainly, but not me. I'm not responsible. Or, am I? The deer followed me, insisting.

I wondered, just what was I responsible for? I didn't change a magnificent wetland into a manmade flood-control project, forgetting that this is precisely the function of a wetland. I didn't pollute it with sewage, trash it with litter, or harm its wildlife. I abhor such things. It is not what I was responsible for, but what I *am* responsible for that matters. The past is not in my power to change. The future can be another matter. I am responsible for teaching what I know, for telling others what I have learned, for helping them to see what I am just beginning to see and they cannot. I am responsible. I am responsible for not keeping quiet, for speaking out, for helping out.

I am responsible for sorting out my own land ethics and sense of stewardship. I am responsible for becoming thoughtful and not merely reactive. I am responsible.

This drastically altered, befouled little piece of nature is perhaps the best we can do for the moment, given where we are. Maybe such a place can become a crack in the collective consciousness of all of us who live so frantically here, a crack that opens up a vision to something better, richer, deeper, more pure. If it has been our destiny to modify our landscapes so drastically, perhaps we can relent and find a way to work with nature to return something of what we so foolishly drove away. We can never go back, but we can work with our landscape with greater wisdom and harmony. We can surrender some of our arrogance and be willing to learn from nature, that master teacher.

Yes, I am responsible. I am responsible to choose my words and to use my words. The deer had disappeared.*

*Since this essay was written, the Cook County Forest Preserve has launched a multi-million dollar project at the Skokie Lagoons to clean up the water, remove rough species of fish, such as the carp, and restock with game fish.

C. Kenney '92

leopard apples

My dog had been stealing apples off the low branches of our dwarf apple tree. Maybe she knew something I didn't. After all, Molly considered herself a connoisseur of apples. A mixed-breed dog, malamute, husky, and blue-tick hound, born in the orchard country of Door County, Molly knew things. Her first love was men, any man. She could spring straight up and plant a delicate kiss on the lips of any unsuspecting six-footer. Her second love was apples, but she was a lot more choosy about them. I couldn't take a bite of apple in the remotest part of the house without her showing up. I swear Molly could tell when I was just thinking about having an apple. Waiting alertly for me to flip her the core of a Golden Delicious, Mac, or Jonathan when I was finished, she would rise on her hind feet and snag the core in mid-air with never a miss. But, if the apple was past prime, she would spit it out and give me that "You've got to be kidding" look.

Molly was "rescued" by my daughter, who came home one day with a tale of a puppy who was the last of a litter and about to be done away with if someone didn't adopt her the next day. I was in an awful spot. I hadn't planned on another dog. So I took this Solomon-like decision out to ponder on my morning run. The words which came to me were, "Let there be life." Although the usual trying times of puppyhood followed, it was a good choice.

The dwarf apple tree came to us much like Molly. Sort of an orphan, it was a rejected anniversary gift my parents returned with a "thanks, but no thanks" response. Taken aback by the rebuff, I had to scramble to find a spot on my own tiny lot. I was now responsible for the fate of this little seedling taken from the security of its nursery. I didn't want to see it die. About the only place available was back in the corner of the yard under the overhang of my neighbor's great-grandfather elm. This was not the most promising site for a young tree, but it would have to do. The seedling was given a home, watered, and that was it. The rest was up to nature.

Not much happened in the first three years. There were delicate pink and white blossoms in the spring, but no fruit. In the fourth year, six small apples appeared, a little miracle! Sadly, as they matured, they became gnarled around tiny brown spots, signs of a hosting insect. To add to their lack of appeal, the big elm tree dripped its fine mist of summer sap on the fruit. Dust and dirt adhered to the film and the skin took on a spotted look. I called them "leopard apples" and left them for squirrel food.

The years came and went with alternating bumper yields and times when there were hardly any. The apples began to stay on the tree longer and get a little bigger. It seemed such a waste not to use them, but they certainly didn't look appetizing. I thought maybe I ought to try spraying the tree and went so far as to buy a simple sprayer and a bottle of insecticide. Just reading the label put an end to that enterprise. What a terrifying experience! Methoxychlor, malathion, captan, and xylene range aromatic solvents didn't sound like something I wanted to put on fruit I intended to eat. And, all the potential hazards listed for humans and domestic animals weren't things I wanted to be responsible for.

The emphasis on extreme hazard for bees and toxicity to fish clinched it. Even the colorful pictures of perfect fruit on the label couldn't convince me that this was a product I wanted to turn loose in the environment. Sure, I have no doubt ingested plenty of similarly treated food products unknowingly. But that was out of ignorance or necessity, a passive acceptance of how things were being done. Somehow, that was different. I couldn't accept becoming an active agent in a practice I thought was harmful. This, I thought, is where the individual can draw the line. Once we first say "no," we can begin to make other decisions. The line can be tightened. We awaken from our trance and start to question the way we are told it must be. We begin to see other possibilities and alternatives.

For the time, the apple tree went on bearing imperfect fruit for grateful squirrels until the year my wife decided to trim up the wild-branched tree for aesthetic reasons. There followed an incredible season of production with branches bowed to the ground like an old man bending to his cane. There were far too many for the squirrel population, so they were able grow to full size in late October. Watching Molly harvest the lower branches made me wonder if I was missing something. I walked up to the tree, picked an apple, and looked it over. The fruit was robust and well shaped, not a sign of the insect which had caused their earlier gnarled appearance. I wiped the skin off on my jeans and bit into it. The body of the apple detonated, sending streams of strong, lively, and distinctive flavor to startled taste buds. What an awakening! Nothing subtle here! My dog knew what was good!

I grabbed a basket with the zeal and giddiness of a forty-niner who had just found gold. The little tree yielded almost a full bushel, and I had harvested them none too soon.

A heavy frost was due, and in a few days the apples would have been on the ground and starting to rot. Few things are so emotionally satisfying as carrying your own bounty into the kitchen. Deep, long forgotten stirrings brought me back to something very basic and made me smile.

When I placed the basket next to the bag of Golden Delicious apples my wife had brought home from the supermarket, I laughed out loud. Those apples were so perfect, so shining and smooth-skinned, they looked like a collection of clones. There was not a blemish among them. They reminded me of the bowl of wax apples my mother once kept on our dining room table. Next to these "store-bought" aristocrats, my apples looked like a bunch of ruffians. If they were displayed next to these perfect specimens and marked "free," no one would take them, except maybe if they had a dog who liked apples. I hadn't really noticed before because I was caught up in the exhilaration of the harvest, seeing the glory and not the imperfections of the crop. Well, just look at them, I told myself, all different sizes and shapes, rough skinned and irregularly colored, how could they have any appeal? Their golden skin was cov-

C. Kenney
'94

ered with dark greenish blobs—mottled frog green, swamp green! Wouldn't you think twice about biting into an apple like that? Well, I had to admit I had.

Looking at them, you could see these apples of mine had character. Why, if you named them you could tell them apart in no time. No two quite alike. At least they scrubbed up well. The blobs of discoloration went away; besides, each had the hint of a rose blush to its cheek. You knew the apple had to be healthy.

Molly was one of a kind too, the friendly face of a husky (a bit heavy on the eye shadow), the curly tail of a malamute, and the long legs with blue spots on the stockings of the blue-tick hound made her a distinctive original. Her aliveness was intense. You could see it in her eyes. I never knew a dog who thrived so on eye contact. She looked right into the deepest part of a person with a question: "Are we going to have fun?" She was also a world-class scrounge. When it came to food, she redefined the word "opportunistic."

Following Molly's lead, I bit into another apple. The flavor came out and wound itself around my tongue. Words like, "WOW!" "ZAP!" "ZAM!" wanted to come out. The true beauty was under the skin. So, to be fair, I sampled one of those genetic wonders of perfection from the supermarket. By comparison, nobody home. Worse than bland: wimpy. So ironic. My "real" apples couldn't be given away, but these overbred royalty bring a nice price. Isn't that just the way it is? We are so seduced by appearances that we have forgotten what substance really is. Above all, look good—fake it and you might make it.

There is no substitute for the feeling that comes from biting into a cold apple off your own tree at harvest time. You could just ask my dog, Molly, except this October there were no apples, and Molly wasn't here to forage for them. Another season of bounty will come. We will remember Molly and smile.

C. Kenney
'94

second floor tenants

*S*tepping out of my cabin door into a bright October morning, I caught an unusual movement out of the corner of my eye, a motion where there wasn't supposed to be one. Something fluttered in the glass bowl of a rusty old lantern hanging on a support timber. Moving in close, I could see the unmistakable scallop shape of a small brown bat's wing. He had apparently slipped into the chimney opening in the early morning and been unable to climb up the slick surface to escape.

Before releasing him from his glass prison, I took advantage of the chance to examine him at close range. While I had watched the bats' nightly air show for years around my cabin with great fascination, this was the first time I ever seen one mere inches from my face. Just as I was beginning to drink in the details of that tiny creature's delicate black mask and anatomy, I noticed there was something else matted to the bottom of the lantern. My brain eventually sorted out the cluster of indistinct fur into the bodies of two more bats. They were not moving. Were they dead? How long had they been there? Alarmed, I quickly pulled the glass bowl off its frame. The active bat left immediately for the forest edge beside my cabin, but his companions remained motionless.

Without thinking, I began to stroke the soft fur between their delicate, mouse-like ears and admire their wondrous structure which allowed them to foldup umbrella-like into such a compact space. This was not a smart move, for had they roused, they might have given me a nip in self defense for my impertinence. Their bodies were not stiff with death. Either they were in a deep tupor or weak from hunger. I had no idea how many days and nights they might have been trapped in the lantern. Nor did I have any idea of what I might do to help them. Years of unexpected encounters with seemingly disabled wildlife had taught me not to rush in with well-intended intervention. Gently, I moved the dismantled lantern to the shaded protection of an old wooden crate, then I retreated, leaving nature her opportunity to deal with the situation. Checking in a little later in the morning, I found that the bats had vanished in the daylight just as they were supposed to do. Relief washed over me, yet I was a little disappointed that I wouldn't get to study my small friends closer.

On my walk down the path through the woods back to the family cottage, I suddenly realized how far I had come from my first encounter with bats in Door County so many years ago.

We had just purchased our dilapidated little cottage in the fall of the previous year. All winter long back in Evanston I had been refinishing and reglazing the broken windows to install the following spring. There was not a single pane that didn't have to be replaced. We knew it was going to be a long restoration job, with only three vacation weeks a year plus a few long weekends thrown in, but we told ourselves it would be luxury camping with a roof over our heads.

I spent the first day happily installing our new windows, finally sealing the cottage from the elements which had roared through it for years. We had a bedspring and mattress for our sleeping bags and a Coleman stove set up on the picnic table on the porch. Our lantern cast strong shadows contrasting with its warm yellow light. There was that good, tired feeling that comes from a satisfying day's work in the pursuit of one's dreams. We were all quite cozy and comfortable as we settled in for the night. The two dogs curled up at the foot of the bed, and Alice, our cat, took up position on the pillow just above my head. With a weary smile, I reached out, turned down the lantern's wick, and settled into the luxurious silence of our cottage in the woods.

Not long after the lantern went out, there began a soft, but persistent sound, one hard to identify, a kind of fluttering and squeeking.

"What's that?" my wife asked in alarm.

"What?"

"That sound!"

"What sound?" I asked, playing dumb and all the while having a pretty good idea who was responsible. I stalled for time, hoping the creatures would find a way out on their own.

C. Kenney
'94

"Don't you hear that?"

"It's nothing. Go back to sleep." By then, however, my courageous dogs began to whine.

"Aren't you going to do something?!"

With a sigh of resignation, I reached for the flashlight. There they were, about a dozen brown bats swooping all about the cottage desperately looking for a way out. I had sealed all their familiar exits with my new windows. The dogs looked on in such wide-eyed amazement they didn't even bark. Flying mice!

Now what? How do I deal with a whole room full of bats? All the old fables and fears came in to "haunt" me. Nasty, rabid, bloodsucking, hair-ensnaring, evil creatures of the night have come to challenge my manhood, and they are winning. Then this valiant knight arose from his bed of fear to defend his family. Brandishing a beam from a flashlight like a mystic sword, and throwing a blanket over his head for a magic cape, he leapt into action. Whirling across the cottage floor, this warrior dispersed the enemy and gained his objective, the kitchen windows. Unlatching them, he flung them open to the black night, then dove back under the covers with a pounding heart. Courage is not acting without fear, it is feeling the fear and acting anyway; right?

Looking back at the incident, knowing what I now know about bats, makes me smile. If the whole thing wasn't so comical, it would be embarrassing. Bats are really quite gentle, helpful creatures. Like so many other animals, they have received a bum rap from the ignorance and prejudices of our European heritage. At the time, I was merely acting out that ignorance. Of course, the bats were grateful to get out into the night and away from the madman. After waiting in the silence for a long time and checking the interior with my flashlight, I made another dash for the windows and shut them. In the interim, a good many of the mosquitoes the bats had gone out to feed upon had come inside to feed upon us.

The twenty-five years following this first incident have brought a lot of changes. Almost yearly work on the cottage had made it much more comfortable and attractive, although it remained on the rustic side. I had changed, too, in many of my attitudes towards the other inhabitants of the forest.

The cottage was still no palace. There were ants in walls, an occasional mouse wintered over, and a family of red squirrels usually spent the winter in the attic. Everybody stayed in his proper space, and we all learned to live and let live.

Had this been our city home, occupied with our city mentality, we might have indulged our hysteria and called for the exterminator, some steely-eyed Arnold Schwarznegger. I can see him now, dressed in goggles and mask, loaded down with traps, cages, and spray canisters, ready to spay a little more poison into our lives in the name of pest control. But this place was our outpost for getting closer to nature, so we learned to tolerate a little less separation. The slight animal scent which greeted us when we opened up each spring was a ceremonial part of the experience. It was easily dispersed by burning scented candles the first few days. And so we lowered our expectations as far as tidy living was concerned and left many of our urban compulsions at home.

Changing my view about bats was probably more of a challenge than it was for other, seemingly less "dangerous" wildlife. A few minutes of reading any objective study of bats should be enough to dispel our historic hysteria. However, our fears and biases are so deep that facts alone cannot heal us. We need to confront our fears more directly with a willingness to experience wildlife in more personal ways.

We have been so thoroughly indocrinated with the ignorance and fear of our much vaunted European culture that we are terror struck by the sight of harmless creatures. And we called the Native Americans ignorant, superstitious savages! They at least understood and appreciated their relationship to the world around them instead of fearing it and trying to subjugate it. Today, other cultures understand

and value the role of bats in their environment and take steps to encourage and protect the bat colonies while we cling to our ignorance. It is ironic that these gentle, intelligent creatures have become the very symbols of horror for us.

Even if you remain somewhat squeamish about bats, please consider the following facts (resulting from the research work of the renowned expert on bats and author of *America's Neighborhood Bats*, Merlin D. Tuttle) before continuing to indulge our popular and misinformed folklore:

1. Bats are not prone to rabies.
2. Bats do not present public health hazards.
3. Bats are not aggressive toward humans.
4. Bats are only likely to bite if handled.
5. Bats make a major contribution to insect control.
6. Bats help our environment by lessening the need for pesticides.
7. Bats are endangered species, and their loss would result in serious consequences for us all.

Living on the edge of a wetland ensures fewer tourists, but many mosquitoes. Knowing that mosquitoes make up the main menu for my local bats, I cheer them on each evening and sometimes accuse them of being slackers. When I consider that just one of these little flying mammals can consume hundreds of my tiny tormentors in a night, it is sobering to imagine what summer would be like without my little mouse-eared friends.

The more I read and the more I learned firsthand from my summers in the boreal forest of Door County, the more tolerance and curiosity I acquired. Nature began to open up to me like a continuous picture book of wonder. Of course, the wonders had always been there; I was the one who had actually opened up. Layer upon layer was removed from my dimly seeing eyes, and I became like a small boy always on the edge

of exciting new discoveries in the world of nature about him. Setting aside my judgments, my urban sophistication, and unfounded fears, I became open and receptive to what lessons and joys nature had waiting for me in her classroom. There was no tuition, no exams, no credit hours, and graduation never came. The rewards were intangible and beyond measure. All I had to do was show up with a certain willingness and receive. Summer vacations became much more than sunning on the beach. I was granted much more than a brief rest; I was made new.

One thing about personal encounters with nature is just how much can be learned, not just about the object of inquiry, but about our-selves. Among other things, we see how distorted our outlook is and how diminished our spirits have become. In order to reperceive the real-ity of nature, it is not enough to simply read about the facts; we need to re-engage. This is not always easy, and I don't suggest you invite your neighborhood bats in for dinner; just entertain the idea that they are unfairly judged and not the loathsome creatures we have been pro-grammed to believe. Try looking again without the judgment.

Consider the old saying that "FEAR is False Evidence Appearing Real." When you face your fears, they disappear. So go out some night and watch the bats with a different perspective. What have you to lose? Unfortunately, many of us seem to enjoy being terrorized more than we do liberating ourselves from old fears. Maybe we just prefer drama over the peaceful state of living in harmony.

One of the simple joys I still look forward to is the big air show put on at dusk by the little brown bats. Hauling a reclining chair out on the deck to face the western sky, I crank it back, relax, and wait. Tall spires of black spruce and cedar stab into soft pink sunset hues of the sky dome, defining the peaks and valleys of a Hollywood set. Soundless flapping of scallop wings appear, vanish, and return. The show has begun. As an aviator, I appreciate the skill displayed in their "aerobat-ics." Their nimbleness puts my noisy, clumsy efforts to shame. An invol-untary smile and chuckle always comes to me at this opening scene. It is so like that of some grade-B horror flick that the bat flights seem downright comical. There is no admission or cover charge to the show, and it goes on all night. Watching the late show against the diamond-dusted, black-velvet drapes of the window to the universe is one of the most peaceful visual meditations I know. And no, I don't wear a hat to keep the bats out of my hair. Their sophisticated method of locating the finest object in the dark, called echolocation, keeps the bats on target.

On the night of last August's "blue moon," I witnessed an all-time great performance. Awakened by the intense light coming through my window at 2 A.M., I went outside into the familiar world, now transformed into something magical. The moon had bleached the balsams, turned the whole flank of the boreal forest silver. Dark cedar trunks framed a lake of wrinkled tinfoil, and luminous bats flashed through openings of moonlight. Filled with the magic of the light, their wings ripped jagged tears in the blackness of moon shadows with unexpected suddenness.

I wondered if I should be seeing all this. Had I happened on to some secret ceremony too pure for human eyes? I felt like an intruder and retreated in my sleepy uncertainty only to later regret not having drunk in more of this rare liquor while I had the chance. Once in a blue moon. Yet, it was enough. The symbolism and image would never leave me. While I was moved by the experience, I doubted I could communicate my feelings to others. It was only light, I argued with myself. Only light! What is more mystical than the qualities of light, more profound than its mere physics—a messenger, a giver of visions. I was meant to attend. I had been called out into the night to learn once again how to look upon my world differently, to see how my own dark places could be torn open by silver wings. The wildlife keep on instructing me.

Last spring the small white frame of a screen lay on the ground under my attic vent. Its rusted-out screen with the big hole in it begged to be repaired. Under the ledge were scuff marks, probably left by the red squirrel who had finally dispensed with this obstacle to her easy access.

I wondered just how many critters I accommodated up in my attic and whether my live-and-let-live policy was a wise one. Did my mosquito abatement crew actually winter over up there, or did they go off to a cave somewhere in a massive nesting colony like they are supposed to do? Didn't know for sure, but maybe it was time to try another arrangement.

So, over the winter I am going to build a bat house or two to be mounted on the tall cedars next to the cottage before I repair and replace that screen. I wouldn't want to lose these valuable allies.

jensen's clearing

*I*n 1974, without really knowing why, I was drawn to enroll in a spring nature study course at a place called simply "The Clearing." I had wanted to shed my city ignorance of nature and learn more about what surrounded me at my little cottage site, just recently acquired. Jensen, who passed away in 1951, had been the founder and resident guru of The Clearing since its inception in 1932. He had been one of America's foremost landscape architects in the early part of this century, and The Clearing was something of a "retirement" project undertaken in his seventies. He called it his "school of the soil," where he introduced his landscape architecture students to their connection with the earth.

The scope of study and inquiry was much greater than the title suggested. He might have just as well called it a school for reuniting man with his natural world. The purpose and curriculum have changed considerably since Jensen's death, but the program still strongly reflects his values and beliefs. Today, it is no longer a school for budding landscape architects, but more of a vacation school offering week-long courses to the general public on the arts, nature, and philosophy.

Heading to The Clearing, I thought I was just going to do a little nature study in a rustic setting. I didn't realize what a clever trap old Jensen had set for overstressed, out-of-touch urbanites like myself. Entering the gate, I encountered a sign announcing The Clearing as a private school for "discovery and contemplation." This proved to be a benign and understated definition. The sign might more properly have said, "Beware of the possibility of powerful transformation."

Jensen was a man rooted in the land as firmly as the cedars clinging to bluff beside his cabin. His own roots were in his childhood experiences on the farm in Denmark, a heritage he honored all his life, even as a big-city landscape architect in Chicago. Even in his advanced years at The Clearing, Jensen was impressive. Full of aliveness, his blue eyes cracking with energy above a white Prussian mustache, Jensen's tall physique and self-assured manner always commanded attention. While

good-humored, he was a man of strong values and opinions and not shy about expressing them. He was a visionary whose principles are now being seen as even more valid today. His deeply spiritual qualities, especially in his appreciation of man's relation to nature, are, in my opinion, what help distinguish his work from mere landscape architecture.

Jensen believed in the "spirit" of the land, much as the Native Americans do, although he came to that belief from a different path. He felt that the native plants and community of plants had "soul," but more than that, they had messages and lessons for us, songs and poetry. He orchestrated this music in his designs, drawing from the healing capacity of the natural landscape to move and comfort the human soul in his subtle, artistic arrangements. One did not have to believe in Jensen's philosophy in order to be influenced by it. One only needed to experience his landscapes to be affected by them. Some of his clients were among the most materialistic, practical-minded, big-money barons of the early twentieth century.

From the first curve of the gravel road into a green world of maple, beech, hemlock, birch, and cedar, I felt something hovering in the woods like a peaceful spirit welcoming me. With each twist of the road, I was taken further away from my old world, much further than the few hundred feet actually involved. I may as well have left the planet as I knew it. I had entered another realm. The roadway was lined with pure-white trillium, some giving way to lavender, with the next act, lovely yellow lady's-slipper orchids, just getting ready to come on stage. The woods presented themselves in layers, from the delicate ground layer composed of ephemeral wildflowers and ferns to the dogwood and young beech understory to the giant trees overhead, contesting one another for the light.

As the roadway weaves through the woods, you can feel yourself changing, slowing, seeing, being enveloped in the luxury of green life accentuated by wildflowers. Then, suddenly, you are delivered to a large open meadow with currents of daisies and golden coreopsis running through it. "Ah, The Clearing," you think, but no, *The Clearing* is a state of mind achieved by merely being in this setting and surrendering to it. Leaving an unpaved parking lot and following a path, you come to a cluster of stone and wooden buildings with cedar shingles and steep-pitched roofs that speak of old Scandinavia. The buildings are gathered along a wide courtyard with a pathway defined by irregular-shaped slabs of limestone well separated by grass borders. Not only are the materials native to the region, most came from the site itself.

The small settlement is rich in plant life. Big maples shade the center, beech and ancient birches define the edges, and shrubs give the buildings irregular borders, disguising what lies around the corners. Wildflowers, choke cherry, and flowering dogwood decorated the building bases and the grounds. No paved surfaces. Automobiles out of sight. The result is a true sense of settlement and tranquility. The main lodge and handful of small dormitories look like they have been there since the turn of the century.

You sit in a sun opening on a cedar bench ringed by the big trees, and you can feel your life quieting down, yet expanding. You take deeper breaths and delight in the aroma of spring woods. A quiet aliveness begins to replace frantic drive. It all feels so perfect, so natural. At first you don't realize how carefully this landscape has been crafted. Of course, the plants and materials are all native, but the introduction of buildings and pathways has been orchestrated in such a way that they flow into the setting with a minimum of disruption. Jensen blended his materials so that buildings, pathways, openings, and vegetation appear to have all grown up together in a harmonious arrangement. The combined effect upon the visitor is one of profound peace. You can feel yourself settle into the scene. There is no TV, no fax, and only one phone. It is a setting in which people naturally become relaxed and friendly . You begin to sense there is something to be learned here about a better way of living. The hand of the Master was everywhere, and so was the hand of the master landscape architect, Jensen, who knew to

work with what had already been created by nature. His art was never obvious. He set a cleverly disguised trap for frazzled urban man, and I fell right into it. I was taken prisoner by his small "community," which lives in close harmony with nature without trying to dominate it.

Following a sawdust trail that undulates through the woods away from the main cluster of buildings, you are led to the "schoolhouse," a long, rectangular, many-windowed building with a high-pitched roof and buttressed wall. Inside, a long, open hall with a highly polished wooden floor is dominated by a twenty-foot-high window made up of twenty-seven separate lights looking out over Green Bay at Ellison Bay Bluff. There is a special feel to the room, a sacred quality. One has the feeling that profound and wonderful things could occur here. It has the feel of a hall of special learning. Simple wooden stools and tables line the walls by the windows, ready for the works of "art" to be born.

Here, as elsewhere in The Clearing, you see the creation of a climate for the expressions of both the practiced artist and "secret" artists. There is a lingering spirit here left by all the good work done by so many generations of students pursuing the discoveries of their own talents. That good energy hangs around long after they have gone and becomes part of the fertile soil in which subsequent students sink their creative roots. It is a quality, that when you are open to it, you can reach out and run your hand over. When you are willing, the special quality of The Clearing can give buoyancy to your creative dreams. This is the place to learn something new, to write your story or poetry, to draw, paint, or carve, play your music, try a new craft, or to free the mind to explore different paths. The Clearing is a nurturer of the creative spirit. Some people come just to "get away," but many come to pursue a special interest, a small dream, to engage in a creative act, that little "art" they always wanted to try—the one an inner voice keeps asking for. "I want to paint. I want to write. I want to create… I want to learn about…."

Blend Jensen's setting with the energy of those drawn here to follow the quiet message of their hearts, add the joy of teachers sharing

what they love, and you have a powerful chemistry, the amalgam for personal transformation. When you arrive, you bring no history. Nobody knows you. You become free to express that inner aliveness of the person you really are. At the closing night ceremonies, the old schoolhouse cackles with the release of creative energy. The Clearing is a school of discovery all right—self-discovery! When it is all over, you wonder what it was all about and what you can take back. This experience is your chance to reassess, reawaken, and pay attention to the things the heart cries for: its own expression of your uniqueness in whatever creative form, to claim it and take it back with you when you return. And, you come away knowing what Jensen knew: that we cannot live fully if separated from nature. He provided a setting for us to experience what we have lost. No sermons required—just open yourself to being there, and your soul responds in spite of your civilized trappings.

C. Kenney '93

cabin fever

Cabin Fever—it's not what you might think, not the crazy-making, long winter confinement in some small space we associate with tales of the pioneers, or even our present-day use of the phrase to denote the desperation to just get out of the house for a while. For me, cabin fever meant the growing passion for having my own cabin surrounded by woods and woodland creatures, to have a quiet space of my own.

Today, on this glorious June morning in Door County, as I sit in my ninety-percent completed cabin (honoring the ancient Chinese proverb, "Man finish house, man die"), I look back on the curious course of construction and see there was much more to this adventure than mere carpentry. There were unseen hands other than my own assisting in this project. There were more "reasons" for my enlistment on the cabin voyage than I knew.

My first exposure to "cabin fever" came from reading Thoreau's account of building his own cabin at Walden Pond. At that time, I was still a young man not many years out of college. I didn't even own a piece of land on which to build, so the notion was merely a fantasy not ready for action. Still, the virus was in my bloodstream, incubating. The idea of a man constructing his shelter with his own hands struck me as a worthy mission. It fermented in my mind and would occasionally bubble to the surface for no apparent reason. Then there was a simple little poem that my eyes fell across in my poetry-writing years. This poem made the spark of connection between my childhood years of building cardboard forts, tree houses, caves, and other hideaways to my adult longing for sanctuary. I no longer remember the whole poem, but its final line said, "If we are lucky, we have them still." It validated my feelings and turned my dream towards reality.

Now I can clearly see how the spirits of men I never met drew me to this site and guided me to create an expression of my own space. The real catalyst was Jens Jensen, founder of a retreat school for the discovery of the arts, humanities, and nature called The Clearing. There, off on the edge of this sylvan site, Jensen built a one-room cabin perched on a bluff over Green Bay. It was his retreat from his retreat. Why he needed to do that was, at first, puzzling to me. It seemed superfluous. Why would you have such a place if you lived at The Clearing? I had yet to learn about the richness of solitude and its power to link our inner selves with nature. Jensen knew what he was doing. He also knew a great deal more about me and my own needs than I did. Following his artful paths, I came to understand how he viewed the world and what I needed to do to survive in it.

Students at The Clearing learn very early about Jensen's little cliff house. They are told they can even reserve an evening for an overnight, if they wish. But, it is clearly not for everyone. In fact, the cabin itself is not so easy to find. Its access is located near the juncture of two trails, one following the top of the bluff and the other a barely discernible path leading from the gravel road. If you weren't looking for it, you might walk right by the black tarpaper roof and limestone chimney just below.

The cabin is settled on a ledge of the Niagara Escarpment about twelve to fifteen feet below the cliff. The "stairway" is a steeply pitched series of stone slabs extracted from the adjacent bluff itself. The only handhold is a cedar tree at the edge with a convenient loop of root protruding from the rocks. After that, you place your feet carefully on each step going down. Such deliberation is appropriate for, without your knowing it, each step has the potential for leading you deeper into your own essential self. The steps lead you away from the distractions and comforts of our social order, even one as simple and gentle as The Clearing, into the depths of our solitary selves. Our culture rarely encourages us to make such journeys. It is this journey into an unfamiliar realm, whether we know it or not, which creates the fear, or the little uneasiness masking the fear, about spending a night alone in a place like Jens' cabin. We do not really fear what may come out of the dark so much as coming face to face with ourselves in the silence without the usual escapes to keep that confrontation at bay. Beyond the terror of our

own silence is an opportunity to gain access to something greater than the "realities" offered within the boundaries of our frantic little lives.

The heavy wooden door swings open with ease on its long, wrought-iron hinges. You step inside and are greeted by the strong scent of spent wood coals. Underfoot is the irregular, cracked slab of the limestone ledge looking like the broken basement flooring of an old house. A portion of the floor is covered by a worn rug of braided cotton. Three of the walls and the ceiling are made of thick, crude planks hewn from heavy logs. Gashes can still be seen from the adz which was used to hack out level surfaces. The planks have the rich, warm tone of dark, unrefined honey. On the cliff side, the wall is composed of thin-bedded limestone slabs mortared together, giving the illusion of being part of the escarpment from which they came. Native timber and stone are in crude enough form to remind one of where shelter really comes from. The heavy timber ceiling beams and limestone wall give the place a sense of enduring qualities. Only ten by fifteen feet, the one-room cabin is the final statement of simplicity. Thoreau would have approved.

Opposite the door, a single window looks down along the side of the bluff, framing tenacious cedars rooted in the rock. The wall facing outward to Green Bay is filled with four long barn windows, each containing eight lights. A small, crude table in front of a double window and two hand-crafted wooden chairs provide the social center and workplace, an oil lamp illuminates the room at night, and a stone fireplace in the corner removes the chill.

For sleeping, there is a rusty framed cot with an ancient pad covered by a rag rug. A personal sleeping bag is required. Two non-functional pieces of "rustic" furniture, a bench and a tall table constructed of birch branches, complete the furnishings. Of course, the wood boxes for the fireplace are essential components. A box of matches, a candle, a can of Off, a dustpan, and a broom are tucked in crevices and corners of the fireplace wall.

All the basics one would need for a few days and nights are pre-

sent, given that public facilities and good, hot food are within a short walk of a few hundred yards. Yet mentally, the world is at a much greater distance than that. All that can be heard are gull cries, the constantly shifting sound of water working on the rocky shore thirty feet below, the wind, sometimes thunder or an occasional passing boat. Each window light frames a separate portrait of combinations of cedar, lake, and sky, and you are left to frame your own mental portraits, as you consider who you really are when set free from artifice.

The setting provides a meditative environment which can help reclaim the soul and deliver you from the world of inconsequential concerns. Gradually, your constant head chatter runs out of opinions on countless things so that the voice of your deep, quiet mind, the one that has waited so long, can be heard. Then you know why Jensen needed this special place, even in the midst of his own temple of nature called "The Clearing." He needed to be away from people, his own students, and his work in a place where he could replenish his spiritual connections without the distractions of his culture. Being alone, yet in harmony with the universe, rich in solitude, recharging and liberating the creative spirit, does not create loneliness; it inspires. You know there is something better you can do, and the search can begin right there.

After having spent several nights and days in Jensen's cabin, working on poetry, communicating with my self in my journal, and peeling off layers of creative dead skin, I knew why he built his cabin. And I knew why I had to build my own. Staying there, I did not think his thoughts; I thought my own. Still, we were one in spirit. Just before leaving, I freed a butterfly trapped behind the window. It knew it could fly, but it was held back by an invisible barrier.

Once the fever to have a cabin in the woods got into my bloodstream, there was no relief. The outcome was inevitable. Perhaps there would be a cure in the distant future, but that was uncertain. The boundary zone between fantasy, commitment, and action is a blurred one. Inching ever closer to the slippery edge of no return, I first chose a site back in the woods on a piece I owned in Door County.

It was a former beach ridge left by retreating lake levels at the end of the last glacier. This swell rises high enough to remain dry during the spring when the swales are full of melt water.

The site is located along an old logging trail which wanders back into the second growth stand of cedar, black spruce, balsam fir, birch, and poplar. A forest fire had swept through in the 1940s, and its path is marked by a thicket of young balsam firs and spruce vigorously competing for the light. My site had a mix of surviving old cedars and new growth, so with a little thinning among the thickets, a pleasant opening with an attractive mix of trees could be created. I began to cautiously clear the site in the summer of 1981.

Once enough room was created, I would take a folding chair out to the site and just sit there looking up at the circle of sky framed by the tall cedars and spruce, listen to the birds all around me and so close at hand. The chickadees, redstarts, nuthatches, ovenbirds, winter wrens, downy woodpeckers, great crested flycatchers, blue jays, robins, and a great variety of migrating warblers flew about me as though I weren't there. Every time I visited the site, it just felt right. I was only a few hundred feet back in the woods, but the curving footpath and the thickness of the vegetation hid me from both the road and the existing cottage — I could just as well been in the heart of the forest.

At first, I thought of buying a small, one-room cabin and moving it to the site, or putting up a prefab storage shed so I could have my private hideaway immediately. I even shopped around for a prefab, but something held me back. Although I wasn't clear on the why of it, I intuitively knew it was more important for me to build the cabin than to merely have it. Even though the project would divert precious time from my writing, there was something in the idea of building that spoke to the creative side of me as well. It was giving expression to creative urges which was important, not the form they took. Building my own shelter with my own hands would be a voyage across unknown waters, an exploration for which I wanted to sign on.

With the surge of this new awareness, I went to Lamperts Lumber Yard and brought back a load of cement blocks, bouncing them in a rusty wheelbarrow over the rough, rolling trail back to the site. Sweating and cursing over stubborn poplar stumps, I wrestled my blocks into place and laid out long lengths of felled spruce trees to mark the outline of the cabin. Then I began to tell friends that I was building a cabin. The ink was on the contract. No backing down now. With that declaration of intent, the doors of assistance opened wide with all kinds of offers: windows from an old farmhouse, help on carpentry problems, and enthusiastic support from family and caring friends. Now all I had to do was build a frame and roof around my windows.

When the Lamperts truck arrived and dumped a load of two-by-sixes at the roadside, I knew I was under way. It was the first of a series of many such sequences and stages of construction where the delivery truck would bury me in materials and I felt a surge of creative excitement mixed with a little hard knot of doubt about just what I was going to do with all this "stuff." This precious lumber was now my responsibility, awaiting my hands to craft it into useful purpose.

The process really began that cold spring morning as I staggered along the trail with twelve-foot two-by-sixes cutting into my shoulders, wading through the swale filled with frigid spring runoff numbing my shins. I had created this cabin in my mind in a vision exercise years before, and now the reality would begin to take shape through hard labor. The assembly of the floor joists gave me a ten-by-twelve platform, the shape and hope of more to come. I would sit out there in the woods and imagine what would follow. Each stage of construction brought new challenges, new skills, new mistakes, and old discouragements. But, when the framing went up, the siding was added, the roof shingled, or the windows fitted in place, the surge of joy and satisfaction would be enough to launch me with enthusiasm towards the next hurdle of construction.

I was no skilled carpenter, only a humble apprentice, a careful

C. Kenney '92

worker willing to learn. Like the Stanley Tools ad, I had the willingness to "help do things right." My "assistants" joked about my passion for careful work, but none of us knew at the time just what the real motivation was. Perhaps when the structure was first closed in, I began to have a more conscious sense that there was a deeper purpose and intent beyond nailing up a little cabin. Although I didn't know it at the time, through my thoughts, care, and intentions, I was creating a "sacred place." Gradually, it became clear that the project was building me as much as I was building it. I would like to say I built my cabin alone, but that wouldn't quite be true. At times, there were the helping hands of friends and family, the encouraging words of fellow writers, and, with such great minds as Thoreau, Jensen, Burroughs, and Jung urging me on, I was well supported in my project. From time to time, a carpenter friend of mine, John Smith, helped me get started on phases I didn't quite understand, or on the two-man jobs such as hanging the rafters, but mostly I worked alone. Watching the sweet-smelling sawdust dancing in the fresh cuts, planing down the perfect fit, hearing my hammer echo in the woods, watching the frame take shape, I was about as happy as a man could be.

Visitors came by. There was almost always the cheerful company of chickadees chirping about my head, encouraging me on. A big, black dog, part Labrador retriever and part St. Bernard, supervised the clearing and early construction phases. He would watch me work until he got tired and then nap on the floor decking. At the end of the day, when I would take a break to go running, he would accompany me and bark at the cars he thought were a threat to my security.

A young, orphaned raccoon, who adopted us, was the most enthusiastic "helper." Serving as building inspector, she climbed all over the framing, in and out of windows, over the roof and up and down adjacent cedars to get a better view. Each day she would check my toolbox for shiny nails and screws or other appealing objects to add to her private collection. As building inspector, she took it upon herself to toss unfastened shingles from my stack on the roof back down to the ground, one of her favorite games. My freshly puttied, six-light barn windows weren't quite up to her aesthetic standards, so she put her own creative stamp on them with her busy little hands. Finally, weary from a full morning's work, she would climb on my shoulders and wrap herself around my neck for a comfortable ride back to the cottage for lunch.

From the very beginning, I found a passion to weave symbols of past lives into my new settlement. Hours were spent laboring on window frames of a hundred-year-old farmhouse. I could have bought complete window units and just plopped them in place, windows which were the latest word in carefree energy efficiency, their trim already painted a bright, lasting white, but no, I had to do it the hard way. I had to struggle removing old paint, scrubbing weathered gray wood with steel wool and oiling the surfaces, turning the clock back on the old oak until it glowed with new life. On one, under the surface, I found the name of the Ellison Bay farmer for whom some unknown mill hand had made the window. Was he a young, blond Swede or a gray craftsman? Either way, he had to be a Scandinavian, just like the farmer. Layers of grit and steel wool coated my jeans and my gloves. I could feel the dust on my lips, a smile too. This was work worth doing. These were values worth preserving.

One of the upper windows is all that remains of a former fish shanty and the other comes from an abandoned barn. My furnishings consist of simple antiques: a cane seat rocker, a small kitchen table with a single drawer, and a high-back engraved chair that once sat at a dining-room table of a Door County farmhouse. An ancient Indian medicine bowl, which holds the matches for the candles, was picked up on the lake shore.

Outside, hanging on the wall, are the simple implements with which men of previous eras hacked out a living from this beautiful but difficult land. They include a shark-toothed, two-man crosscut saw of a

C. Kenney
9/93

logger; the hay scythe, potato shovel, oxen yoke, and pitchfork of a farmer; and the fish box, floats, and twine net of a fisherman. These implements are not for cute or rustic decoration; they are symbols of another time to remind me of how privileged I am to be a tenant on the land where all I have to do is honor it and celebrate its beauty, not scratch out a living. These artifacts connect me with the past and make my site a link in the stream of settlement. They were chosen purposefully, shown reverence and respect, and given a place of honor.

I can't say when the cabin will finally be "complete" or exactly when I considered it habitable. Probably the latter came about three years after construction began when it was first closed in. Since that time, a few pieces of furniture have been added, and pieces of writing have been produced. Following this work, my wife and daughter presented me with a carved wooden sign proclaiming the cabin as the "Word Shop." As I look about me this Fourth of July, 1994 and see a missing piece of window molding and an unfinished loft, I feel no sense of urgency. Recalling that Thoreau declared his own cabin finished on the Fourth of July, I smile and reflect on the significance of this date for personal independence.

My cabin measures only ten by twelve feet, a squarish little box with a high-pitched roof which overhangs a small deck at the entrance, giving just enough cover to sit protected if the rain is coming straight down. Above the door hangs my "Word Shop" sign; above that, the only north-facing window. It helps put a little light in the loft. Rough cedar board eight inches wide covers the exterior, while the inside walls have the reverse smooth cedar siding up to a height of four feet with rough white plaster above. Two thirds of the ceiling area goes straight up to the peak. The remaining third is loft area. There are no windows on the west wall, and the only one on the east is in the corner looking down the worn, winding footpath to the cabin. On the south is where the windows are concentrated. Three generous windows are arranged in pyramid fashion to let in as much light as possible. They are meant to

C. Kenney '92

capture moonlight as well as the sun. These windows look out at the thicket of young forest with its pinnacles of older spruce and cedar towering above and stabbing at the sky.

Under the upper window hangs a wooden plaque of a sprinting fox inscribed, "Fox Lair." Beneath the plaque is mounted an antique oak mirror positioned just above the one-drawer, maple kitchen table. In the corner sits a handmade carpenter's tool caddy with handles protruding at odd angles. Two sets of crude shelves hold boxes of nails, lanterns, candles, rocks, books, and miscellaneous items. It takes constant surveillance to keep unneeded things from creeping in and establishing residence.

As yet, there is no wood-burning stove because I would have to sacrifice a large cedar tree no matter which wall I used, so a small propane space heater fills in on chilly days. Not the same. The choice is hard.

On my walls hang carefully selected items of personal significance. A cluster on the west includes a deerskin drum, a dream catcher, an outrageous feather mask, an inlaid wood portrait of a wolf, and a deer skull. On the opposite wall are mounted navigation charts of my two favorite bodies of water: Puget Sound and the waters around the Door County Peninsula. Between them hangs a mandala blessing them both.

A small bulletin board is mounted on the wall and contains many pictures of airplanes flown and ones yet to be flown, masses of planes at Oshkosh, a picture of writer-friend Marcie Telander caressing a horse, and a poster of a bare tree against a brilliant full moon saying, "Limits exist only in your mind!" Above the door is a small poster of a seascape, a cloudscape, and a single gull given to me by my daughter when I started the cabin project. It says, "Dreams are wings for the soul. Let your dreams soar!" I remember when she gave me the poster and reaffirmed my feelings for the place. We put the ladder up and climbed up to the loft. We sat up there on a small square of plywood flooring hugging our knees like two small children celebrating the discovery of a neat hideaway.

Now, looking out the window at my feeder table four feet away and at the wall of the forest another thirty feet away, watching the parade of birds and other wildlife, I recall the words of John Burroughs' famous quote about his own place, Riverby: "The most precious things in life are immediately at hand, without money, without price."

The sense of completion grows each year with the small details which slowly get handled—a little trim, some staining, the hanging of a mandala or dream catcher—but the single most satisfying act of completion was the replacement of a modern door acquired late one season in desperation for a way to close the place up for the winter. I hated that door from the beginning. That wimpy hollow-core door of thin veneer, the kind you find in new, cheap housing, the kind you could put your foot through if you were in the mood. For years this imperfection grated on me. Then, in 1993, with a big remodeling project going on at The Clearing, I was able to acquire a solid, thick, tongue-and-groove cedar door. Bolted with cross braces and equipped with a simple wrought-iron latch, it was a perfect match for my rough, cedar-sided cabin. The heavy door swung easily and shut with the quiet authority of old Jensen himself. That token was all that I needed to complete the spirit of the cabin.

Now, as I write these last few lines by light of a big white candle and think about how building this small abode has enriched my life over so many seasons, I see that creating the cabin as my sacred place was the real purpose. Walking into the cabin and closing the door is like entering a meditation chamber. The quality of quiet is as pure as spring water, the peace palpable. So rich is this peace that, at first, it can be sampled or endured for only short periods of time. Marcie Telander wrote me from Crested Butte, Colorado, offering congratulations on my project. She told of her own experiences in returning to her cabin after months of travel. "Sometimes when I sit in my cabin and look at the Englemann spruce, the mountains, and a world full of snow, I am peacefully overwhelmed. Sometimes I feel that it is all I need. And then I write."

Having a sanctuary in which to write became a secondary benefit. In his memoirs, the famous psychologist C. J. Jung tells how he created his own retreat from the modern world by building a stone tower where he could live simply and reflectively, a place where he felt connected to his life, his ancestors, and his own creativity. Every four years, he would add to his building until it became a reflection of his inner workings. Perhaps that explains why I will never actually finish my cabin and why nothing ever goes into it that does not have a particular meaning.

I have been blessed by following my intuition about my cabin project. It has led me down a rich path of learning on many levels, even when I didn't know where I was going. Now I understand more fully the why of it all. In John Burroughs' words about his own Riverby, "I come here to find myself. It is so easy to get lost in the world."

C. Kenney '92

creating the clearing

I am drowned in the aroma of pine needles piling up in springy boughs lying all about me as I behead the crown from each long trunk. My delirium mounts in the warming sun of new light as I stagger through a mine field of fresh stumps staring up at me in shock. Sweat pools in my glasses, and my arms shake with fatigue. It has been a glorious and lustful campaign. My hands are sticky with sap that will not come off, and I begin to wonder about the conflicting passion and guilt. What was the origin of such primal feeling? Did it matter? The deed was done. My clearing was in place, but how had I come to this juncture?

When I first came to this forest/lake edge, bought an abandoned cottage to restore, and established my foothold on the land, I was both naive and cautious about making any changes. So in awe was I of this green density seemingly undisturbed by man, that I was reluctant to remove, cut, or even trim any living thing.

In the beginning, such restraint, in view of my ignorance, was a good thing. In time, such a laissez-faire policy would prove impractical and unsatisfactory, but it was better that I learned a few things before picking up my ax and saw. Several years passed before I could bring myself to take down the big, dangerous white cedar slowly tipping on a trajectory toward my cottage roof or pull up the swarms of young balsam firs crowding the walls or cut back the poplar clones screening my view of Lake Michigan. It even troubled me to reopen the old logging trails for my explorations back into the interior of the wild cedar wetlands. Considering my urban background, it is hard to say where such an ethic came from, but it was like some ancient, dim memory that whispered to me, "Walk lightly on the land," and I had to obey that call.

Seasons came and went. I watched, studied some, and slowly learned a few things about the wildlife, vegetation, rocks, and limited cultural history of my chosen place for summer retreats. The more I learned, the closer I wanted to become to all that was around me. A yearning for intimacy was kindled, and it became a hunger for more and more, deeper and deeper. Knowing the names of wildflowers and birds was not enough. I sought a kinship, a belonging.

My bias against clearing was challenged when I decided that the cottage was too full of children, dogs, and cats to give me a peaceful place from which to contemplate nature and do the writing I professed to want to do. Besides, the cottage was too close to the road. I wanted a quiet "blind" right in the thick of the forest, out of sight.

I chose a former beach ridge just two hundred feet back along an old logging trail. This stony ridge gave me a dry site safe from the spring melt waters. There was just enough room between a couple of big white cedars to fit a small cabin without removing any substantial trees, just a few saplings. And so began an eight-year project of learning and building.

More tranquility could be found in this little building than my urban soul could absorb. Each season there was always a period of transition required from city life before I could let in the gift of peace. But my forest blind was too complete. The forest closed in on me just ten feet from my window with a density that hid all beyond that point. Thickets of balsam fir saplings crowded in on one another, sometimes just inches apart, their horizontal branches interlocking arm in arm, forming a dark mesh which neither body nor eye could penetrate. Only their topmost branches gained enough light to support a few scanty fronds of flat green needles.

Almost everything below eight feet was shade pruned. The slender trunks and twigs were coated with gray-green mosses and lichens. Competition among species and individuals was so intense, none seemed to be gaining or benefiting. Scrawny, long-legged, misshapen, struggling for light and space, they looked like those photographs of starving humans taken to elicit support for hunger drives, not what one might think a healthy forest might look like. I knew that I was imposing my own aesthetic judgments and the tangle I was seeing was characteristic of a cedar wetland, but I needed to modify some of the competition to

achieve my own goals for the site without corrupting it. There were no Christmas-tree shapes on the balsam firs; they crowded about the knees of big black spruce and white cedar like a swarm of unkempt children obscuring the classic form of these more dignified-looking trees. One had to look up high to recognize faces in this crowd. Here and there a sickly poplar or skinny birch had managed to twist an emaciated trunk through the thicket up to the light and present a few leafed branches to the sun, with the inexorable balsams slowly gaining on them.

My eye could catch movements in the thicket and my ear told me that redstarts, nuthatches, chickadees, white-throats, and winter wrens were about, but discerning species by color or seeing detail was impossible. They eluded me in that tangled-mat backdrop. If I were to see, admire, and learn from this outpost, there would have to be space; there would have to be light. I needed a clearing if my little site was to function like Jens Jensen's Clearing (a clearing of the mind through becoming one with the landscape). I would have to step up and take responsibility for managing this little patch of forest before my eyes. For one who respected the natural world and wished to merely leave it be, such a decision was not easy. Who was I to decide what would live and what would die? There had to be some philosophical context for my actions or they could become wanton mayhem. How would I choose what to cut, what to leave? How could I reconcile my actions with my values?

It had been my good fortune to have taken a forest resource-management course the year before and to have participated in prairie and savanna restoration projects as a volunteer. I had begun to understand that my direct involvement in selective cutting was not "a crime against nature," but could have beneficial results. I came to acknowledge that it was acceptable to intervene for my own benefit as long as it was done with restraint. I was a disturbance on this site, but so was the forest fire which swept through here fifty years ago. If I was to be here, engaged with nature, I wanted to meet my needs in thoughtful, less destructive ways, to engage in accommodation without domination. I am this edge creature who needs light and space, a transition into the thicket of forest whose floor could only support mosses. I needed this zone where I could live in harmony, in contact with the creatures and vegetation of this habitat around me, a space where I could interact peacefully.

My theme became: let there be light. My goal became one of creating light and space to encourage the full expression of the major trees on the site, to bring light to the forest floor for the boreal wildflowers, to aid some struggling species to survive, and to keep the wonderful diversity intact, to see what might evolve in a small space. With the succession clock restarted on an even playing field, who would show up, prosper? I wanted to create avenues for the eye into the forest for a sense of depth, for sightings of creatures, and for narrow passageways into its secret places.

I wanted to create corridors of light to let the sun slip through the canyons between the tall cedars and spruce, let empty space define their spires. There would be no economic gain from such "management," only the pleasure of assisting, observing, and learning.

And so I began, slowly at first, sitting for hours staring out of my south window at the thicket, focusing upon burled trees I wished to exhume, deciding which saplings and young trees to remove, making my apologies to the lichen-encrusted sticks of balsam fir which had to go. It was murderous work best carried out quickly once the decisions had been made, but not in the spirit of attack. I had to beware of the pioneer zeal for clearing, beating back the enemy. That blood also ran in my veins and had to be kept in check. Just a few saplings cut at a time, return to my window, look again, think again. Be humble, be thoughtful, be deliberate. You are this clumsy giant given dominion, but not wisdom, not knowledge.

Back and forth, sawing, chopping, clipping, pulling, looking again, and gradually the classic shape of cedar and spruce emerged. I could see the red squirrel scamper over the forest floor. Light returned

to my deck once a strategically located poplar came down. The forest gloom dissipated, and my stack of long, thin poles grew deep. Each trunk was trimmed of its lateral branches and arranged by size. My hand ax gave off a satisfying "ping" with every dry branch clipped. Still, there was an almost inescapable feeling of shame connected with all this slaughter in spite of my reasoned intentions for the site. Only by treating the harvest of this clearing with respect could I absolve myself.

What to do with all this scented bounty lying at my feet? Let some return to the forest floor to rise again. A bundle of big fronds would go for my ceremonial fires at my sacred place at the beach, fires with the power to sizzle away the stars, then bring them back again. Balsam needles could be stripped and collected to fill small pillows with fragrant reminders of this place on dreary winter days in the city. And all those tall poles, what would I do with them? I could build a hut, a secret place even deeper in the forest as I had wanted to do when I was a kid. It could be for my grandsons or the kid still living in me.

Now, as October ends, the work is done. I have taken mindful action and will wait to see how nature will respond. I can sit on my crude bench and feel more a part of the forest because I can see into it for a distance in places. I made an offering to my neighbors in an aluminum pie pan filled with sunflower seeds. They came almost immediately, without fear or even much notice of me, to feed at my feet. The chickadees and nuthatches arrived in abrupt, swift flight just past my ear, the sound of their little wings like a deck of cards being shuffled. They hit the pie pan with authority on tiny wire legs and were gone in a flash. A chipmunk peered over the edge of the deck and then went about filling his cheek pouches. Trilling from the closest cedar, a red squirrel invited me to leave, but failing in that, made jerky advances and retreats like a mechanical windup toy before deciding to help himself. The gray squirrel, however, was serene and confident, as though this feast was set just for him. My pen lay idle, the ceremony of closing up the cottage and the cabin for the season went neglected, while I was content to conduct open house. At night the cleanup crew went to work as a fat raccoon put away the leftover sunflower seeds.

Open house was a great success. The creatures of the forest came closer to me than they ever had before. I felt as if I belonged to this place. Yes, I belong to this piece of land; it has claimed my labor and my love, but it does not belong to me. I am a mere apprentice on the land, not its ruler. I am a tenant on a season-to-season lease of unknown duration, just another passing figure like those before me. I keep their artifacts hanging on the cabin wall to remind me, to keep me humble: the Menominee mandala, the forester's bucksaw, the farmer's potato shovel and scythe, the fisherman's net, fish box, and floats. These men are all gone and I am just the next character on this stage, a set piece for one more scene on the drama of the land.

old cedar

*J*ust a week past Easter, and I stood with my hands jammed to the bottoms of the pockets of my thick Eddie Bauer jacket, shoulders hunched against the chill of a damp wind off Lake Michigan, wondering why I had come north so early in the season. Door County has little to offer in the way of awakening nature at this time of year. I could have been out pedaling my mountain bike, wearing a T-shirt, and admiring early spring blooms if I had remained in Evanston. But, like the Canada geese, I always grow impatient to return north as soon as the thaws begin.

So there I stood outside my shuttered cottage, staring at the bare piece of ground next to it where my old cedar deck once was, remembering. I remembered how my dad insisted we build that deck almost a quarter of a century ago. There I was with a long-abandoned, dilapidated cottage to make habitable for my growing family, and he wanted to build this damn deck first! I had just barely finished removing the collapsing ceiling, shoveling out the red-squirrel nests, ushering out the bats, and glazing the shattered windows and he insisted we build a deck next. Well, there never was any arguing with a man who was so accustomed to doing things his way and always won out. Besides, for what I was paying him, he could choose his own projects.

I smiled, remembering the big lumber truck from the old Lamperts yard in Sister Bay pulling up with stacks of two-by-six cedar planks and a load of heavy concrete blocks. How we had struggled with those blocks to align and level them in place—twisting them down into the unyielding stony soil to lower them a quarter of an inch or filling in with dirt and stone to raise them a shade so the bubble in the level floated between the marks. Dirty, frustrating work before the fun began.

How fresh and clean that lumber looked, all stacked and ready to go. The aroma of the cedar intoxicated us with a zeal to build. All day our hammers rang, driving big zinc-coated sinkers into the sweet wood. The sound of good work being done. The two of us often saw the world through different eyes, and our styles were not the same, but on that day there was a silent harmony in our movements as the creation of the deck evolved between us.

Later, I had to admit the old man was right. The satisfaction of building this clean, new structure gave me the energy and inspiration to tackle the nasty inside work of rehabilitation. So many times over that summer I would stagger out from the plaster dust, insulation material, and paint fumes to drop my tired body into a tattered lawn chair, put my face up to the sun, and breathe that spring-pure Door County air. I would thank the old man for his wisdom about the deck and smile at the thought that he still had something to teach me at seventy-two. That deck became a refuge, a solid friend, a family gathering place, a viewing platform for the lake and forest edge, and a reviewing stand for the parade of neighbors down the road.

That was a long time past, and a whole new era was beginning. Dad had died a year ago at Easter, and, after so many seasons in this damp boreal forest, the old deck had grown dilapidated with decay. Cedar has marvelous qualities that resist rotting, but not forever. The old cedar had stood strong in spite of never having had any preservative treatment, but now the joints were soft, the ends crumbling with dry rot, and the rusted nails wobbled in their holes.

The fungi were laboring hard to return the wood to the forest humus for its next cycle of life.

Last October I had reluctantly allowed a friend of mine to dismantle the deck as payment for a week's stay in the cottage. Somehow, I could not find the heart to do the job myself, nor did I want to witness the work. So there I stood looking at the stack of weathered boards growing green moss colonies on their ends and laced with white mycelium like the wispy streaks of an old man's hair, remembering. Concrete blocks stood askew like markers in some neglected cemetery, and the remains of the deck lay awaiting my decision for disposal. I wondered if perhaps it would not have been better to have everything taken care of

C. Kenney
8/93

last fall so I would not have to face dealing with these pathetic witnesses to the past. Then I could start all over again as if there had been no past connecting me—pretend—at least until the hammer rang out again.

Slowly, I turned over each board, still wet between layers from melted snow, a dampness accelerating decay. I sighed as I laid them out to dry and poked at the soft places. Towering all around me, looking over my shoulder, were the spires of the great-grandfather cedars, survivors of storms, fire, and man. Back when this area was first logged, white cedar was not considered to have commercial value due to its tendency to split; therefore, many of the larger trees were spared. Now, the wood is highly prized and is being rapidly cut. My little reservation of tall cedars still holds out.

How many majestic cedars had fallen to the forest floor to build my deck? You don't see them crashing down when you look at neat stacks of lumber at the yard, just as you don't see the slaughter of the Hereford when you order a burger. We are removed from the real price of our choices. Yet we must choose, and all things, including ourselves, must die, just not before it is time and not without respect, not without reason. In choosing, we need to remain conscious of the consequences of our choices.

What did all these thoughts mean for my rotting cedar boards? What was I supposed to do with them? Cremation was unthinkable. There was still life beneath the dying surface if I had the will, the strength, and the patience to extract it. The fate of these precious boards was in my hands; this resource became my responsibility, although I had wished it to be otherwise. The elders stood around me in silence, seeming to watch with folded arms.

What possible use could I make of this near-lifeless lumber? Perhaps I could build a foot bridge over the swale on the trail leading back to my little woodland cabin, the one which runs with such painfully cold water in early spring. I could saw off the rotted ends, cut eighteen-inch planks, buy some new long joists, even use the concrete blocks for piers. But, did I really need a bridge for such a short wet season? At least the idea of trimming, planing, sanding, and excavating the life out of these gray forms began to excite me. And I could hear the admonition of Grandma Jackson, as I so often did, "Waste not, want not." Yes, that ringing affirmation provided just the inspiration to ignite the drive to find new life for my charges.

It was not time for this cedar to die. After all, is it not called *arbor vitae*, "tree of life"? Whether so named by the early French explorers for its healing qualities against scurvy or because of its remarkable ability to survive in two such different environments—thin, impoverished stony soils and sphagnum moss on the low, wet shore lines, or the high limestone bluffs of the Niagara Escarpment over Green Bay where they struggle to find a precarious root-hold in the rocky crevices—does not matter. There is a tenacity of character that makes this tree the very symbol of life. In its classic form or contorted shapes, tipped or erect, the cedar seems to possess a dignity and spirit of survival.

It was decided. If I had to saw these planks down to one-by-twos to salvage something, it would be worth it. Cedar grows too slowly, has too much worth and dignity to be cast away carelessly simply because one can "buy" more. My campaign to save the cedar began.

On a walk through Jens Jensen's famous "school of the soil" known as The Clearing, I spotted a design for a rustic wooden bench situated at strategic locations: trail heads, overlooks, and quiet, wooded nooks. Yes! That would be a perfect retirement role for the old cedar, and it would honor the memory of the work my father and I did together. A bench for the beach, a couple for my cabin site back in the woods, others scattered at the junctions of old logging trails where I could wait for wildlife to come to me instead of stalking and disturbing. Maybe even a rustic bench for a friend or two who would appreciate its origins and give it a home for their declining years. Ah, the fever of it all! I had an industry; the cedar had renewed purpose.

After the planks had a week of drying flat in the sun while I took measurements, calculated angles, laid out patterns, and marked off rotted ends, I was ready to begin. My crosscut saw ate the pencil lines while cedar sawdust danced out of the cut, bringing back that distinctive scent.

Chickadees sang around me from the branches of the balsam firs. The sun warmed my back, illuminated my work, and made the early trip up feel worthwhile again. As I planed, cut, fitted, and nailed pieces together, I keep hearing, then singing, the old Shaker song, "'Tis a gift to be simple. 'Tis a gift to be free." Where that came from, I couldn't say, but it was the most natural and perfect expression of my feelings. Nothing more was needed, no elaboration. It was complete.

Complementary angles met, and twelve pieces of old cedar came together to become a rugged, simple bench. The very character of these boards made them appropriate back in the woods; no silken gray tone, no smooth skin—rather roughness, age spots, and knots, all speaking to the unpampered life. Yet, with each cut, fresh faces appeared sweet and pure and unchanged inside, brightening my own imagination, inspiring new purpose.

Next I found the bench would not work on the irregular ground behind my cabin, so another use suggested itself—a small deck. I had needed a platform back there from which to view the forest and its wildlife, a small raft to float upon in sunlight surrounded by a deep green sea of forest. This structure would not be "son of deck," but reborn as the father of all my decks, smaller now, rustic and isolated, contemplative in its old age. Weathered hide, strong heart, seasoned, grown closer to the land, nearer reuniting to the earth, providing a place of thoughtfulness away from the curious eyes of the road, a place to be a part of nature, not apart from nature. There was an inaudible grunt of approval from the surrounding ancient ones.

More sawdust flew, its scent rekindling youthful optimism about meaningful projects. My saw sang, and so did I. My hammer was the only sound in the forest, and when it grew silent there were two crude modules more or less four by eight each. They were propped up to level on small slabs of limestone from the floor of the 350-million-

C. Kenney
9/93

year-old seabed beneath my feet. There was just enough room for two benches placed at right angles in one corner and an apple crate between them to hold the coffee or the wine. They could sit there like a pair of old cronies keeping each other company in the sun of their last seasons. The opposite corner had space enough at a polite distance for a pan of goodies for company.

I had just arranged the "deck furniture" and settled back with a sigh, arching my stiff back and stretching my legs, when two reddish brown blurs in close tandem cut the bias across my deck, red squirrels. How appropriate those nervy rascals would be first! This was going to be a good place for my retired cedar to start a new life. They would be surrounded by their kind, respected for their worth, and would assist me to learn and to see what is really important.

fox

*L*ate one night, comfortably settled in my makeshift basement den, I was peacefully reading Loren Eiseley's *The Night Country* when I was suddenly ambushed. I had been escaping the mind-numbing, debilitating effects of yet another dreary, adversarial public meeting of our local city council, which my job as city planner required me to attend.

Reading Eiseley was cleansing my soul from all frantic nonsense I had been exposed to over the past few hours. There was nothing trivial about Eiseley; he was a man of depth and substance whose writing style was a pleasure to read. I trusted him to deliver me from my overexposure to the theater of the absurd. But this evening he ambushed me.

On page three, without warning, he suddenly stripped me of my disguise. It was as though all four of my limbs had been snared and the strong cone of light under which I had been reading became a glaring spotlight. All the world could see. All the world would know. In just a few simple words he called me out. Although Eiseley was speaking about himself when he said, "The fact that I wear the protective coloration of sedate citizenship is a ruse of the fox—I learned it long ago. The facts of my inner life are quite otherwise," those words rang like an alarm for me.

He went on to describe the events in his own life that had led him to take up the tactics of the fox, but I was barely listening. My mind was darting about in the bright light looking for a place to hide. In time, my wild mind calmed down and admitted its identity. Although my history was different from Eiseley's, I, too, had become a runner of civilization's fence lines. I had been a fugitive learning to survive in a world alien to my values and beliefs, avoiding discovery. Where were my people, my culture? Had my tribe left me here by mistake? The solitary, secretive fox survived in many guises, looking out from behind the mask, alert, learning their ways, always knowing everything that went on 360 degrees around him, being able to move silently without detection. Fox adapted to this harsh urban environment but kept an untamed heart.

C. Kenney
6/93

At first I struggled a bit with this totem, my masculinity uncomfortable with such an androgynous image. Why not Bear, Wolf, Eagle, or Mountain Lion? They were not me, that is why, and this totem had nothing to do with my masculinity. So I surrendered to the truth about this appointment, accepted it, owned it, and opened myself to learn what there was to learn. Still, I was slow to admit this secret identity to anyone. Who, in this world, can a fox trust? Then there came a time of personal crisis when I sought the answers to my own identity through one of those intense California workshops. The first assignment was to discard your name and choose a new identity for the next ten days. Without hesitation, I wrote "FOX" on the name tag.

Without expanding on the details of this workshop, it became an opportunity for me to turn inward and to discover more about the real me as differentiated from the me I had been told I ought to be. Fox became validated and accepted by others. He was set free on a vision quest to become who he really was. That time laid the foundation for a powerful, personal transformation. An animal had given me the symbol I needed to initiate my own quest, and once I had acknowledged the secret fox in me, he began to show up in my life with regularity. My close friends readily accepted my "new" identity as fitting and even started calling me "Fox." Fox figurines, greeting cards, pictures and articles began to appear in the mail. One friend, intimately familiar with the Native American way, sent a "vision" tape she created especially for me and provided the spiritual linkage for which I had been searching.

Most remarkably, the foxes I had wanted to know about gradually began to show up in my life. Not long after the workshop, I found a gray fox at the steps of my Door County cabin retreat when I arrived in the spring to open it for the season. He had only recently died, apparently of natural causes, and was still quite beautiful. As the Native Americans might do, I took it as a sign, a rather disturbing one at first. What was the meaning? Why had this fox come to die on my doorstep? Was it a forecast of some dark fate for myself? The image haunted me for months. Then it came to me that the message was a reminder to not let the new-found fox in me die. I had built this cabin that he might live, see, and experience this woodland edge habitat through fresh eyes and to write about it. This fox would require support, protection, and nourishment if he were to survive and not return to the world to become domesticated.

A few years later, I found a second dead fox, this time a silver fox. His black coat fooled me at first; I thought it might be a small dog, but its teeth gave it away. Again, I took it as a sign. My writing had not progressed and now the "silver" fox had died. Time was running out for me if I was to do more than just soak up the joys of my engagement with nature and wildlife. An additional theory occurred to me. Perhaps it was the quality of the energy and intentions that I consciously brought to this setting that had drawn these creatures to a place where they could die. Fanciful speculation? Maybe, but it had a ring of truth that felt right to me.

Over the seasons, I had caught glimpses of Reynard running across Door County meadows at dusk, or crossing Appleport Road fifty yards ahead of me while I was out for a morning run, but aside from my deceased messengers and a couple of pathetic caged creatures, I had not experienced a fox close up. I had seen his purposeful tracks in the snow following the fence line, seen his burrow in the abandoned gravel pit, but never looked into the face of a fox. Tantalizing evidence and fleeting sightings ignited my appetite. How could I draw the living fox to me?

Late one afternoon I was tilting back on my old cedar bench against the south wall of my cabin, just enjoying the gentle sunshine of early spring and taking in the tranquil view of my small clearing ringed by cedar and balsam fir trees. The chickadees had cleaned off the last of the sunflower seeds from the small wooden table just in front of me, and the little nature show appeared to be over. I was totally at peace with no agenda or need to be doing anything other than what I was doing right at that moment.

Out of the corner of my eye I caught an unusual movement. It was an undulation snaking down one of those low animal trails under the balsam branches, an undulation of gray fur. At first, it was unrecognizable, with its head down and in the darkness of the undergrowth, but as he entered the clearing, I could see it was a gray fox. From his relaxed behavior, swinging his nose back and forth just inches above the ground, I could tell he was out on a scavenger mission, sniffing out opportunities. Completely absorbed in his work, with the slight breeze off the lake at his back, the fox was unaware of my presence. I remained still, stopped breathing, and began to feel chilled as he came nearer and nearer. Finally, when he was directly in front of me crossing at right angles not more than fifteen feet away, I realized he was not going to see me or even become aware of my presence.

Resisting any temptation to reach for my camera and not wanting this moment to pass so soon, I took a breath and very softly said, "Hello, fox." He did not sprint for the forest cover just a few yards away as I thought he might. Instead, he froze in mid-trot. It was as though I had snared each of his four feet at once. Then, he turned his head to look at me. I didn't move; he didn't move. We just watched each other intently. He seemed to say, "Okay, you have me; what are your intentions?" We stayed like that for a long time without him showing any signs of trying to run, so I risked speaking some more, short phrases widely spaced. He flinched slightly each time I spoke, but still kept looking at me. I told him how beautiful he was, that I was also a fox, that he need not fear me, I thanked him for showing himself. I spoke in soft, even, respectful tones and not in the silly, ingratiating way we speak trying to befriend a dog. I even told him that if he wanted to leave now it was okay. What he got from that conversation is hard to say, but eventually he came to see I was no threat, because I had him at serious disadvantage yet made no aggressive move.

At last, he took a few tentative steps away, glanced back at me, then returned to his previous task of checking out the ground for

promising scents. He did not trot off for the nearest cover when "freed." He maintained his original direction and purpose. Only when I whistled softly did the fox pause and turn to look at me again. Eventually he blended into the thicket of young firs and was gone. I still didn't move, just sat there letting the waves from the backwash of this moment continue to lap at my mind until all was still once more. What a privileged encounter this had been. I held the lingering sensations lightly as a bubble for as long as I could. I did not rush off in search of witnesses with whom to share the experience. There rose inside me this buoyant sense of lightness. My heart was saying, "Thank you."

Just a few days later, seated on the screen porch of my cottage facing Lake Michigan, I was enjoying that first cup of coffee and letting the early morning rays warm my face, when the fox came again. This time, he was walking down the middle of the road that separates my land from the lake front. When he was opposite me, he stopped and looked directly at me. He seemed to be saying, "I see you there with your coffee, watching me. You may have fooled me once, but not today." After staring me down for awhile, he casually resumed his morning walk down the road, having delivered his message that he was not afraid of me. We had taken one another's measure and would coexist in this territory. Although the season was ending, and I would soon be leaving, I had the feeling there would be future encounters and communication. Yet, I was such a novice. I felt so humble, so clumsy touching a realm that was foreign to my culture and belief system. Was I really capable of drawing the fox to me? What was the meaning if I could?

The winter which followed, far away from Door County, was as much a winter of the mind as it was a season of darkness, snow, and cold. My work withered down to a dry, brown, lifeless form, not unlike the wildflowers and grasses of winter. There was no heart for the writing, only mechanical movements from day to day, doing only just what must be done and waiting for the thaw. In search of an experience which might stimulate the flow of creative energy, I returned to the place at home where I first reconnected with nature. Then, as now, I was more drawn to the spot than making a conscious decision about going.

The site which had been so magical for me decades ago was just a scruffy strip of forest preserve following a polluted, green stream: Harms Woods and the North Branch of the Chicago River. Squeezed on both sides by the development of Chicago's northwestern suburbs, this little haven is all that is left of what once was around where I live. As abused and overtaxed as it is, this corridor of nature still survives supporting native plants and wildlife as well as those who come seeking the experience of connecting with something they don't completely understand.

As I lifted my heavy boots out of the deep snow, laboring with every step, I questioned myself about why I was there. An inner debate ensued, but a deep, determined wisdom won out over the whining of the ego. I began to remember how each of those little journeys had been like leaving the planet for a while and returning restored. Eventually, I made it to the stream, which was still open and flowing in spite of the cold. The upstream effluent-treatment plants keep the water temperatures abnormally high. I climbed atop a giant, fallen willow tree whose trunk was aligned with the riverbank. Brushing off the fresh snow and finding a hollow just the right size for the coffee thermos, I settled in to see if the old magic would return. Of course, my earlier trips had usually been in spring when the woods were coming alive, not in the dead of winter. My clumsy arrival at the riverbank had frightened off a flock of mallards, the only visible wildlife around. Now there was only the white stillness and the slight lisp of the current flowing by.

Without much to look at, I began to recall how it had felt coming here years past. Usually, it was Sunday afternoons when a kind of desperate craziness would hurl me out of the house in search of "something" fulfilling. Time would be running out on the weekend, and soon I would be back at my desk handling countless demands. The break from the job had not renewed me. The opiate of endless sports on the

C. Kenney
194

TV didn't work; watching someone else's high-energy experiences never satisfied my own need for aliveness. Going to the woods always worked. With each step deeper into the woods, I would feel a difference, body and soul. Tiny details which were at first unnoticed began to emerge, and subtle sounds of life became perceptible. I literally came to see and hear again the beauty which was all around me. I took notes, learned the names of plants and wildlife, so that we could become more intimate. The world of man receded to be replaced by the peace and harmony of nature's design. No one ever told me what was out there in the woods; I was merely drawn to them without knowing why. I never questioned the magical cure; I just gratefully accepted the gift.

So, here I was once again seeking in the old place so long forgotten, waiting for the lesson. Jets on their approach into O'Hare screamed overhead and the traffic crossing the Lake Street bridge kept up a steady background of noise. Nothing else seemed to be going on. My tail was frozen to the log, and my hand had formed an icy claw around the cold coffee cup. I began to doubt the guidance which had brought me here and question the wisdom of my frigid patience. Then I began to hear the soft rapping of a hairy woodpecker on the bark of an old oak instead of the scream of jets on their final approach to O'Hare. I would be patient. I would be quiet and wait.

My reward was greater than anticipated. Once I gave myself up to my surroundings, a red fox appeared from behind a brush pile on the opposite bank just downstream from my position. His full winter color against the white backdrop of snow made him a candidate for one of those unreal photos in *National Wildlife*. Oblivious to my presence, he came in a quick trot right past me and up the bank on his purposeful mission. I didn't move, still letting the image fill my mind. Then he was back again in the opposite direction. He knew where he was going and what he was doing, unlike that frozen, drab blob perched on the willow across the riverbank. The message was clear. I saw the circle of life, the returning to this place, the fox messenger again, the need for me to return to my own purpose in spite of my personal winter and write about Fox.

The question I would like you to ask yourself is: "Who are you?" Who are you in your connection with wildlife? Are you the Crow Woman, Bear, Coyote, Wolf, Salmon, Dolphin, Gull, Dove, Eagle, or even Chipmunk? What can you learn about yourself from such totems? What does it mean to you? Are any of these creatures your personal symbols, messengers, mirrors, guides, or instructors? Are they yet one more of the infinite ways in which the Universe tries to communicate with us about who we really are and why we are here? Do they help us claim our true identity from the false personas we have crafted to help us survive in a world we see as unfriendly to our true natures? Can the creatures we identify with help lead us back to our own identity and to sanity, away from the soul-killing artifices that rob us of our expression of our true selves? My answers are in the affirmative. What you will find is up to you.

Richard Carter is a geographer by training and city planner by profession who recently left that practice to focus on his interests in nature and the environment.

He is also an aviator, air photographer, published poet, and writer who has been looking to combine these skills and passions into work which will contribute to the preservation and restoration of natural areas. Recently, he has been doing post-graduate work in environmental studies at Northeastern Illinois University.

For the past thirty years he has been spending summers exploring nature in Door County, Wisconsin, as well as searching out natural havens in the Chicago metropolitan area. As a writer, Richard Carter has been integrating his environmental interests with native American spirituality and personal encounters with nature in order to create new perspectives for himself and others.

about the author

Carolyn Kenney's artwork reflects a lifelong love of and involvement with art and the natural world. Her preferred subjects are the near and familiar—wild creatures, things, and places with which she has had a direct personal encounter.

"We have a relationship," she says. "And when I look deeply, really see what's there, I find new things in what I'm drawing, and in myself."

The drawings in this book represent both a new adventure and a homecoming. From exhibitions and graphics in Milwaukee's natural history and art museums, her career path has led to advertising art direction, a master's degree in business management, and, in 1986, forming a graphic design company. Her recent venture into nature illustrations has provided a joyful expression of her reconnection with the wild.

An amateur naturalist and enthusiast in landscaping with native plants, she lives and works in Wauwatosa, Wisconsin, with Ace the Wonder Cat, Founder/CEO of WonderCat Graphics; feline assistants Kipling, Nicholas, and Trillium; and Smidge the mouse.

about the artist

C. Kenney '92

artist's notes

Title page: Wild bergamot or beebalm *(Monarda fistulosa)*. The lavender flowers of this fragrant member of the mint family are common along Wisconsin roadsides, and in prairies and meadows of varied growing conditions.

Page xix: Woodchuck *(Marmota monax)*. Feeding and/or sunning above ground only one or two hours each day, the woodchuck spends the rest of its time in its burrow. Its strong clawed feet make it an expert digger, and excavation is its specialty. Its home often consists of a system of tunnels with multiple entrances, and may be part of a connected cluster of burrows. There the woodchuck, or groundhog, hibernates from fall until late January to March.

Page 3: Feathers found beachcombing at Newport Beach State Park, Door County, Wisconsin.

Page 6: Cattails *(Typha latifolia)* along Lake Michigan beach, Appleport, Door County, Wisconsin. The fuzzy brown seedheads of this common wetland species are spread widely through wind, water, and wildlife. It also travels through fleshy rhizomes that store nutrients each fall before the upper stalks wither and send up new growth in early spring.

Page 9: Double crested cormorants *(Phalacrocorax auritus)*, flock in a characteristic flight pattern skimming over Lake Michigan. The name *cormorant* is a French derivation from the Latin *corvus marinus,* or "sea crow."

Page 12: Double-crested cormorant *(Phalacrocorax auritus)*. Cormorants migrate in V-shaped formations, like geese, but are silent. The tufts on the crown of this species are seldom visible in flight.

Page 15: Wildflower meadow, Ellison Bay, Door County. Queen Anne's lace *(Daucus carota)*, spotted knapweed *(Centaurea maculosa)*, and black-eyed susans *(Rubeckia hirta)* quilt the roadside meadows along Garrett Bay Road.

Page 19: Red-tailed hawk *(Buteo jamaicensis)*. The red-tail may hunt flying low or from as high as three hundred feet, able to spot small prey below with its extraordinary eyesight. Its huge eyes, which occupy as much space in its head as its brain, have muscles that appear to permit rapid refocusing in flight, much like a zoom lens.

Page 21: White-tailed deer *(Odocoileus virginianus)*. Long legs and jumping ability, sensitive hearing, and a superb sense of smell equip the deer for a quick escape from danger. Extra layers of fat from fall feeding and an insulating coat of hollow hairs filled with air provide protection from winter weather. Its metabolism also slows, and it does not move as much or range so far, so that it saves energy and actually can survive on less food.

Page 25: White-tailed deer *(Odocoileus virginianus)*. Except during the fall mating season, bucks and does tend to lead separate lives in loose clusters of males or groups of females and their fawns and yearlings. In deep snow, they may gather in "yards," especially white-cedar stands that provide food as well as a natural windscreen. Each individual can spend more time feeding and less on surveillance and have access to a common network of packed trails that provide easier, safer travel.

Page 29: White-tailed deer *(Odocoileus virginianus)*; antler and track. Even in areas where deer are common, their shed antlers are rarely found. Because of their high content of calcium and other nutrients, they are quickly devoured by mice, voles, and squirrels.

Page 31: Branch of black willow *(Salix nigra)*. Largest of the willow species, the black willow often has multiple trunks, straight and leaning. It is common to wetland areas, along stream banks, lake shores, and flood plains.

Page 35: Trees lining a quiet eddy along the upper Des Plaines River.

Page 39: Black willow "bridge" *(Salix nigra)*. With the erosion of river and stream banks, great willows often tilt or fall into the water, continuing to grow and sent up new trunks.

Page 40: Great blue heron *(Ardea herodias)*. Drawing its head and neck into a sinuous curve, the heron stands motionless, waiting patiently for a school of fish to swim past. Then it drives its dagger-like bill down to snap one, flip it up, and catch it with ease.

Page 43: Pussy willow branch *(Salix discolor)*. Often found on streamsides, lakeshores, and in wet meadows, the pussy willow is best known for plump flower buds that open in late winter/early spring, revealing soft silvery hair.

Page 44: White-tailed deer *(Odocoileus virginianus)*. The size and number of points in a buck's antlers in fall are an indication of nutritional status and the condition of its habitat, not the animal's age. The strongest, healthiest animal is best equipped to compete for an area or a particular doe and most apt to reproduce and pass on its genes.

Page 47: Vegetation along upper Des Plaines River; tree trunk chewed by beaver *(Castor canadensis)*. The beaver fells trees to feed on the leaves, twigs, and tender young bark of upper branches and to cut the branches into manageable lengths for building dams and lodges. It does not actually eat the inner bark, only chips it away in cutting. It takes less than ten minutes to fell a three-inch-diameter tree, though it may work for hours on a large one. Removing shoreline trees lets in sunlight that favors new growth of more tasty shrubs and saplings and seedlings that have been held back under a closed canopy.

Page 48: Beaver's head *(Castor canadensis)*. Perfectly adapted for water life, the beaver not only has waterproof fur and webbed feet, but also furry lips that seal in back of their chopping teeth, flapped valves on ears and nostrils, and transparent eyelids. Its body is tolerant of high carbon dioxide levels, and an air passage separate from the larynx allows it to breathe while carrying branches when swimming.

Page 51: Great blue heron *(Ardea herodias)*. At four feet tall, the elegant great blue heron stands straight and still. But if approached, it will first extend its long, graceful neck, then unfurl its six-foot wingspan, and push off on its long, springy legs into a slow, measured departure.

Page 55: Black willow *(Salix nigra)* tree stump in water at Skokie Lagoons. Even in urban park settings, dead and/or fallen trees provide shelter for turtles, frogs, salamanders, and small water snakes.

Page 57: Great blue heron *(Ardea herodias)* in flight over Skokie Lagoons. The great blue heron is most often spotted near dawn or dusk, swooping past or fishing in the shallows of lakes, ponds, or rivers. At a distance, it can be easily recognized in flight by its slow, steady wing-beats and the S curve of its neck.

Page 59: White-tailed deer *(Odocoileus virginianus)*. While deer are expert at silently dissolving into the woods, they may snort or grunt if startled before bounding away with a flip of the tail. Or they may stand watching back for several minutes, making a breathy whistle before running. Fawns bleat to their mothers.

Page 63: Pair of "leopard apples" from Richard Carter's dwarf Golden Delicious tree.

Page 66: A cluster of "leopard apples," ripe for picking.

Page 69: Richard Carter's dog, "Molly."

Page 71: Little brown bat *(Myotis lucifugus)*. The little brown bat is a mouse-eared bat, unlike other species whose nose and ears come in fantastic shapes. All bats are fully adapted for flight through finely developed wing and tail membranes, body shape, slender limbs, and furless wings, and can only hop awkwardly on the ground. In straight flying, the little brown bat moves at speeds up to forty miles per hour, with about fifteen continuous wing strokes per second. However, its erratic dodging, diving, and turning patterns make it seem even faster.

Page 75: Antique lantern outside Richard Carter's cabin, Door County—a "cabin-warming" gift from neighbors, the Shays.

Page 77: Little brown bat *(Myotis lucifugus)* catching moth. Bats track and catch prey through "echolocation." Flying in zig-zag patterns, the bat emits a series of ten to twenty high beeps per second and reads the sound waves that echo back when they strike something. Increasing its transmissions to 250 calls per second, the bat is able to judge the size, speed, and direction of its target by comparing the frequency of the echo with that of the beep it sent out. With precision, it sweeps the prey into its veined tail membrane and catches it with clawed feet.

Page 80: Little brown bats *(Myotis lucifugus)*; evening "air show." Most bats feed on insects, though desert and tropical species eat fruit or prey on small fish. Most active in the hours around dawn and dusk, a single bat may consume up to one third of its body weight—as many as 500 mosquitoes or 150 larger insects—in one night.

Page 85: "Council ring," overlooking Green Bay; The Clearing, Door County. Circular stone benches with fire pits in the middle are an element of landscape architecture that Jens Jensen consistantly repeated in his designs. Here one can stop to rest, enjoy the view, or build a fire and watch the sunset or northern lights over the water.

Page 88: Winding entrance road with large-flowered trilliums *(Trillium grandiflorum)*, The Clearing, Door County. The swinging curves of an unpaved road slow and gentle the arrival of students and visitors.

Page 91: Central courtyard, with main lodge and rustic dormitories, The Clearing, Door County. The site at The Clearing was shaped from 129 acres of native woods and abandoned fields. The main lodge and surrounding openings are positioned to take advantage of morning sun in the winter and provide a vista of the sunset behind a trio of huge white pines.

Page 93: Hermit thrush *(Catharus guttatus)*. One of finest songsters of North America, the hermit thrush nests on the ground or in low bushes and feeds on insects there in the breeding season. Unlike the other spotted thrushes, it overwinters in the northern states, living on buds and berries.

Page 95: View through a side window in Jens Jensen's Cliff House; The Clearing, Door County.

Page 99: Twisted cedars cling to the edge of the precipitous stone steps leading down to Jensen's Cliff House; The Clearing, Door County.

Page 101: Richard Carter at work in Jensen's cabin; The Clearing,

Door County. Students and visitors often pause to write at the rustic desk in the Cliff House, and a recent class at The Clearing donated a special journal for this purpose.

Page 105: Red-breasted nuthatch *(Sitta pusilla)*. While red-breasted nuthatches may come to a bird feeder, they are most often seen climbing easily up, down, and around the bark of trees in search of insects. Along with other overwintering cavity-dwelling birds such as chickadees and woodpeckers, they help control leaf-eating insects, consuming some fifty per cent of adults, nymphs, larvae, and egg masses.

Page 106: "Rocky," Richard Carter's tame raccoon *(Procyon lotor)*. Raccoons have a highly developed sense of touch, and their five-toed paws are as sensitive as humans. Foraging at night "by feel," they swirl their palms along the bottom of a pond or stream and poke their fingers into crevices with their eyes fixed elsewhere—a technique called "dabbling." Their ability to learn and problem solve allows them to exploit a wide range of food resources.

Page 109: Richard Carter's cabin in Door County. Like this book, the cabin has evolved with refinements and details. Such labors of love are never done, only ready to use, show, or share.

Page 111: Eastern chipmunks *(Tamias striatus)*. The chipmunk divides its time between dodging predators and food gathering. Its speed and familiarity with escape burrows and other cover are crucial for survival, as is its ability to collect cheek pouches full of food for the winter. Not a true hibernator, it sleeps deeply but intermittently, and so must eat. A bedside supply of food eliminates the risk of exposure to cold and hungry hawks and weasels.

Page 115: Northern white-cedar stump and roots.

Page 119: Grove of balsam fir trees *(Abies balsamea)*. The balsam firs and spruces of the boreal forest share spire-like profiles and sloping branches that allow snow to slide off without breaking branches. Both are well adapted to living in the shallow soil overlying ancient bedrock, with wide-spread root systems that keep them from toppling in the wind. An easy way to tell the two apart is that the cones of the fir point upwards, while those of the spruce hang down.

Page 120: White-throated sparrow *(Zonatrichia albicollis)*. Favoring dense hedgerows and thickets, the white-throat is known by it's plaintive whistled song,"Old Sam Peabody, Peabody, Peabody." Among sparrows it is best identified by its well-defined white throat patch and yellow lores (the area between the eye and the upper edge of the bill).

Page 123: Red squirrel *(Tamiasciurus hudsonicus)* on log. The feisty red squirrel occupies a position in the northern coniferous forest like that of the gray squirrel in the eastern deciduous forest, though their ranges overlap. Solitary and aggressively territorial, the red squirrel constantly chatters and chases other squirrels out of its space. Other intruders are greeted with a loud alarm call and rapid tail waving from a tree or high post.

Page 127: Northern white-cedar branch *(Thuja occidentalis)*. Also known as the *Arbor vitae* or "tree of life," the northern white cedar has flat branchlets of overlapping scales, branching profusely to form lateral sprays. This species is a favorite of browsing deer and rabbits in northern forests.

Page 131: Grove of northern white-cedar trees *(Thuja occidentalis)*. Slow-growing but long-lived, a mature white cedar reaches forty to fifty feet, its trunk often lobed or buttressed at the base. The flat, connecting ridges of its bark are gray to reddish brown with streaks of orange.

Page 135: Red squirrel *(Tamiasciurus hudsonicus)* on cedar bench. Like the chipmunk, the red squirrel seldom stops to eat, concentrating on storing up a cache of food. In northern and transition forests, its most active time is from 4 P.M. to 8 P.M., while the chipmunk typically feeds from 9 P.M. to 1 P.M.

Page 136: Rustic cedar bench and deck; Richard Carter's cabin, Door County.

Page 139: Kit fox *(Vulpes macrotis)*. Though of the same genus as the red fox, the kit fox is actually a desert species of the Western United States. Its body is the smallest of the foxes, with ears proportionately much larger, serving as a means of radiating excess heat. The swift fox *(Vulpes velox)* is slightly bigger and native to the Plains states.

Page 142: Gray fox *(Urocyon cinereoargenteus)*. On average, the body of the gray fox is slightly shorter than the better known red fox, and its skull a little shorter and broader. Its upper coat is grizzled, with reddish legs and feet and a distinctive black mane and tip to the tail. The only canine that regularly climbs trees, it uses sharp, curved claws to pull and boost itself upward, as well as to jump from branch to branch.

Page 145: Red fox *(Vulpes vulpes)*. The genus of the red fox is actually different from that of the gray, though identification may be confused because of several different color phases in the red, including black, cross, scorched, silver, silver-gray, and yellow. But habitat is the telling difference, because the red fox avoids dense forests, choosing areas that combine open woods and edgelands, fields and farmlands. The gray is found in hardwood or mixed hardwood/coniferous forests, especially in the vicinity of rivers and streams.

Page 147: Red fox *(Vulpes vulpes)*. Though the fox is a true member of the dog family *Canidae*, it shares many features with the cat. Dogs and cats have a common ancient *Miacidae* ancestor, but fox/cat similarities are likely due to convergent evolution, i.e., common traits from adaptation for the same task, in this case, hunting rodents at night. The most notable of these is the vertical-slit pupil, combined with tissue inside the eye, called the *tapetum lucidum*, that reflects and multiplies incoming light.

Page 148: Red fox *(Vulpes vulpes)*. Foxes are principally nocturnal, active from a few hours before dusk to a few hours after dawn, depending on how long it takes to find food. They most often sleep in the open, using their dens only during the breeding season. Their range is estimated at one to five square miles, depending on the season, habitat diversity, and food sources. Within this area, they have a network of paths linking areas of intensive use.

Page 151: Red fox *(Vulpes vulpes)* walking through trees. Foxes also exhibit cat-like behaviors, especially when hunting. They stalk in a low, creeping posture and walk by "perfect stepping," placing each hind foot silently in the spot of the preceding forefoot. The stalk is followed by the surprise "mouse-leap" attack: the twitch of the tail, the spring into the air high above the prey, and the landing with both front paws on target.

Page 159: River otter (Luter canadensis). The webbed feet and muscular, streamlined body or the river otter are ideal for all water-related circumstances—belly sliding for play or travel through the snow, wet grass, or mud, as well as swimming. In addition, its nose and eyes can be shut watertight to dive, and the eyes are set high on the skull so it can readily scan its surroundings. The otter typically makes its den along the water under a fallen tree or rocky ledge, in a old beaver or muskrat lodge, or in the bank itself.

BIBLIOGRAPHY

Benyus, Janine M. *The Field Guide to Habitats of the Eastern United States.* New York: Simon & Schuster Inc., 1989.

Benyus, Janine M. *Northwoods Wildlife: A Watcher's Guide to Habitats.* Minocqua, Wisconsin: NorthWord Press, Inc., 1989.

Bull, John, and John Farrand, Jr. *The Audubon Society Field Guide to North American Birds: Eastern Region.* New York: Alfred P. Knopf, 1977.

Grese, Robert E. *Jens Jensen: Maker of Natural Parks and Gardens.* Baltimore: The Johns Hopkins University Press, 1992.

Henry, J. David. *Red Fox: The Catlike Canine.* Washington, D.C.: Smithsonian Institution Press, 1986.

Jackson, Harley H. T. *Mammals of Wisconsin.* Madison, Wisconsin: The University of Wisconsin Press, 1961.

MacDonald, David. *Running with the Fox*. New York: Facts On File Publications, 1987.

Neelands, R. W. *Important Trees of Eastern Forests*. Atlanta: U.S. Department of Agriculture, Forest Service, 1974.

Robbins, Chandler S., Bertel Bruun, and Herbert S. Zim. *Birds of North America: A Guide to Field Identification*. New York: Golden Press, 1966.

Smith, J. Robert and Beatrice S. Smith. *The Prairie Garden*. Madison, Wisconsin: The University of Wisconsin Press, 1980.

Stokes, Donald W. and Lillian Q. *A Guide to Animal Tracking and Behavior*. Boston: Little, Brown and Company, 1986.

Tuttle, Merlin D. *America's Neighborhood Bats*. Austin, Texas, University of Texas Press, 1988.

Whiteman, Ann H., editor. *Familiar Trees of North America: Eastern Region*. New York: Alfred A Knopf, 1989.